the blank screen

by

William Gallagher

The Blank Screen

Cover and photography by: William Gallagher

Dark Ride Publishing

10 9 8 7 6 5 4 3 2 1

ISBN-13: 978-0-9926569-1-1

theblankscreen.co.uk
Email: william@theblankscreen.co.uk

Give feedback on the book at:
feedback@theblankscreen.co.uk

Dedicated to Angela – as am I.

But this one is also dedicated to my mother, Grace Gallagher, who has often wondered what I do for a living. I'm not certain this will really explain it, mind.

Contents

Introduction

This is what it's about: being a productive writer is easier than writing. To Do lists, calendars, phone calls, all of the stuff you have to do when you're a writer is a pain and a chore but it's still easier than facing that blank screen.

Nothing in this book will improve your writing. But everything in it will give you more time to write. I can only say I'm sorry: you're going to get more time in front of that glowing white screen. Glowing screens, white A4, yellow legal pads, Moleskine notebooks, the thing is that they're all empty and you've got to fill them with your talent and your time.

You know, though, that there are moments when you can write like a demon and moments when you couldn't manage to order toffee off Amazon. We do tend to press on when that happens because we feel we should be writing and unfortunately what sometimes happens is that we write so little or we write so badly that it all dents our confidence in our work or in ourselves and makes us less keen to come back to the keyboard.

The ideal would be to recognise when this happens, preferably to even predict ahead of time when it probably will, and not go there.

Often or even usually, though, you have no choice but to continue because you're on a deadline or because you're having to do this in the one ten-minute period you've managed to scrape out of your day. If you could make more time for your writing and also know when these bad patches are coming, you could afford to walk away. Write another day, another hour, after another coffee or whatever it is that gets you back on form.

More, if you spend that same time doing the piddly easy stuff on your To Do list, you've got those done and they won't take up the time when you could be demon-writing.

The Blank Screen: Productivity for Creative Writers is all about making time and using it the best you can. It certainly applies to full-time writers but it may even be more use if you are writing alongside a normal day job. What you learn here will help with that day job too, no matter what it is, and that will mean you spend less time worrying about your job when you're away from it.

Of course, if you're a writing parent with a day job then you're screwed.

I don't have children – I'm a civilian – so I'm no more going to give you advice about parenting than I am going to attempt to improve your writing for you. Parents more than anyone will find it hard to block out certain times to write but at least you'll learn how to see when those best times are for you. It's a pretty good kind of 'at least' too because it will make you happier. Seriously. When you know that you can't write in this minute and you see what else you can do that will give you much more time later, you will be happier.

Honestly. My wife Angela Gallagher once told me that I seemed lighter since I found ways of handling my workload. She said it right after one of those huge changes you get in your working life when abruptly I lost one big client and was having to work on many new, overlapping projects that individually were complex, took a long time and were hard to manage. I didn't realise it until she said it, but she was right. She is right. I love working and I am an incurable writer yet now I relax more because I feel I can. I know where everything is, I know I'm doing what needs to be done and I can know that at this moment it's not just okay to be having a drink, it's the right thing to do. Of course, you're standing there by the fridge with a Pepsi Max and you get an idea.

But I've even got you covered there, albeit because I'll show you how superbly and efficiently I fail to write those down.

That's one case where you shouldn't do either what I say or what I do. But there are other cases too. Don't do everything in this book but try it all. Give it all a good go: most of it takes you some time and habit-forming before you start writing me glorious testimonials about how much better your writing life is. Hint. But I really want you to be as productive as you can be and as creative as you are: when you find something here that works for you, do that. Stop reading. Do that and get it into your life. Then when it's second nature and really helping you, come back and read on for the next thing.

You get to really exploit productivity ideas that truly work for you and I get credit for writing a book that lasts you for ages. Everybody wins.

I have done everything in this book bar the Jerry Seinfeld technique. (You'll see why it's the one thing I don't need.). I continue to do most of it and it works for me. So all of what you're going to read comes from my personal experience. Much of it was also invented by me. But a lot of it is stolen goods. When I tell you about something I didn't invent but know will help you, I'll tell you where I got it. Of course I will: there are very clever people out there and they deserve their credit. But they also deserve your attention and, if it comes to that, your cash. What I feel is that if you are really taken by an idea I happen to have read first on a website by David Sparks or Merlin Mann, they should naturally get the credit but I must also give you links to them. When you like one of someone's ideas, I think you'll probably like more from them and I'll point you the way if you don't already know it.

So there's a section toward the end here called *Stolen Goods* where I lay it all out for you. It's kind of an acknowledgements section too as, though I've not met any of these people and they've never heard of me, their work has helped mine.

I should say, as well, that software has helped me gigantically. But I'm a Mac user and if you're on a PC then my advice is a fat lot of good to you. Some software is so useful that I'm going to tell you about it anyway but unless it applies to everywhere, unless it's platform-agnostic, I'll keep it brief. A reassuring amount of it does work everywhere, so that's good, but where I've been unable to stop myself talking about some Mac or iOS app that I live in, I've gone to enormous lengths – i.e. asked on Twitter – what the best PC or Android equivalent is. So I'll be pointing you at either what's definitely great or what is reportedly great. It'd be a huge help if you'd let me know how that goes.

But listen, this is a book about productivity so we do rather need to start getting productive. It kills me to say this, as a thorough computer geek, but first of all you're going to need pen and paper.

William Gallagher

Section 1

Think of it this way

Most of this book is about showing you which button to press and what to say: it's about the specifics of becoming more productive and staying productive. But for it to stick and for it to all be something you use every day, you need more than tips and tricks, you need to get why it works.

When you do really see why this works then it's the principle that will tell you whether all this is likely to be useful to you or not. Look at this as sizing up what I've got to say and then if it helps, dive on in to the rest of the book and its detail.

This section is therefore the least detailed but it is also the most important one to read. If you were only to read this, it still would help you. You'd just be on your own about how to apply it.

These chapters cover what I think are the key issues in facing the blank screen and I know that they are the points that changed my working life.

Hand on heart, I already knew one of them. The other two issues were hard for me yet now that I get them – and use them – I'm struggling to see why I didn't always.

Chapter 1

Change your mind

You know the idea that women can multitask and that men can watch football? I think it's really that women get landed with too much to do and men somehow don't. Because, while I hate saying this, the truth is that nobody can multitask.

Or perhaps I mean nobody should. But definitely, while the idea goes against the grain and makes me bristle, it is certain that multitasking does not work. It doesn't work for anyone but most especially it doesn't work for writers.

I worked in radio for a time and I can see me there, talking away on air while watching the clock in front of the mixing desk, showing off a little to the colleagues in the next studio, and riding the faders on the record playing so that I could dip the volume to say something more and bring it back up again in between sentences. It really was a record, too. This was pre-CD. Maybe I wasn't multitasking: maybe I was just young. But in those days there was more to do: all the jingles and stings and ads and trailers came on carts: blue plastic carts about the size of an eight-track – look, I don't actually remember eight-tracks, stop it – and I had this thing where I couldn't just take it out of the rack and pop it into the slot on the desk, I had to do it with a flourish. I have no idea why. This is another reason to feel I was very young, though this time I'm more happy that it was a long time ago.

I'd twirl that cart into the desk, announce the time, fade out the current record, stab at the cart button to play in the jingle and sometimes, just sometimes, exactly as I was speaking, I'd get a voice in my headphones from the next studio saying what they needed me to say next to start their show off.

It was bliss.

There's a scene in the film *Broadcast News* where William Hurt's character has just had a similar experience and he describes it as being better than sex. I could confirm or deny but this is a family book.

Here's the thing. Right or wrong, embarrassingly young and showing off or talented radio professional with flair and great dress sense, I did that and I did it well enough that I believed I could multitask. And I multi-tasked like mad. Throw anything you like at me, I can do it all right now. I'd certainly juggle To Do tasks: if I were calling someone then while their phone was ringing, I'd answer an email. I think I was actually trying to recapture that vibrancy I felt in radio but I was definitely convinced that I was getting the work done brilliantly.

I swear my mouth just crinkled up as I start to tell you this, as I start to admit that I was wrong. I did a job once with a US property guy named Saen Higgins and he did that kind of nodding shake of the head that patient people do. And then he showed me.

I think he said he got this from *The Myth of Multitasking*. That's by Dave Crenshaw: if you like this point, take a read, he's got an entire book full of them.

Dave Crenshaw's Multitasking Exercise

Here's his thing. We're going to do something trivial and then do it again while multitasking.

You'll need paper again. When I say go, you should write this line:

"Buy more books at theblankscreen.co.uk"

Then immediately underneath it, number the letters. 'B' is 1, 'u' is 2, 'y' is 3 so underneath the word 'Buy' you'll have written '123'. And you carry on to the end, squeezing the digits in as you go. This is what you'll end up with:

"Buy more books at theblankscreen.co.uk"
"12345678910111213141516171819202122232425262728293031323
3435363738"

And you'll have struggled to fit it all in too. I counted the spaces as well: you can't fault me for thoroughness but it's up to you how diligent you are with this one. But it's the job that's important and the job is to write the sentence, then underneath it write the numbers.

If you can time yourself doing it, do. Stopwatch on your phone or an eye on the clock, either's fine. We just want an idea of how long it takes.

Go.

How long did it take?
You raced at the end there but your time doesn't matter yet. Just do make a note of it.

Turn the paper over. Now you're going to do exactly the same thing, but multitasking. This time, you won't write the first line and then do the numbers, you'll swap between them. You'll write down the letter 'B' and only the letter 'B'. Then you'll immediately write '1' underneath.

Next, you write the letter 'u' and rush to write '2' underneath it. Next it's 'y' and '3', it's a space and '4', 'm' and '5', and so on. Letter, number, letter, number.

Reset that stopwatch, look again at that clock.

Go.

Ready
I don't know. You've got that conscientious face but there's also a bit of wicked sparkle in your eye. Be honest: did you do the exercise or just read on to see what happens? If you didn't do it, then it almost doesn't matter because you're smart, you can see that it would take longer to do the multitasking version. And you know that's my point. But I think you need to do it to really feel the difference. I can't remember what times I got when Saen showed me this but I very much remember the shock of how much slower I was the second time. And I remember resenting it, actually. What I couldn't do was deny it.

Once more, I got this from Saen Higgins and he got it from Dave Crenshaw: you can watch Crenshaw run through this on YouTube.

I'd like to add something to Crenshaw's exercise, though. I think he proves rather inarguably that at least some multitasking can't be done or is much slower than doing the two. But you did write both the phrase and the line of numbers, you got them done, so slower or not, you still got there. You got the same result in the end. However, I think when you're a writer, it's more serious. I think things are worse than he says: I think it's very easy to fail in a task if you're a writer trying to multitask.

So let me try to prove my own theory. I call this addition of mine, The Red Elephant Experiment.

The Red Elephant Experiment

Without making any notes yet, I want you to read a passage of prose that I'm about to make up on the spot. You're going to read it slowly because I want you to read one sentence and then stop.

Read a sentence, turn away and write down a random number between 1 and 100. Then turn back to the passage and read the next sentence. The number isn't important: you could go get a coffee instead, but I need you to interrupt your reading and do something else, do some serious multi-tasking, in between every sentence.

So read a sentence, write a random number, read a sentence, rinse, repeat.

But there's just a little bit more. I'm telling you this going in: I will be asking you three questions afterwards and I specifically want you to be looking for the answers. So much so that I'm just going to tell you the questions right now:

> What is my favourite type of food?
> What is my firm's phone number?
> What colour is the elephant?

Got all that? Read a sentence, write a number, look for the answers.

Here's the passage:

> I didn't notice the elephant at first. We were on the Serengeti and I was thinking about the dark chocolate brownie recipe I was going to use. I've never made anything before but the idea of a continuous supply of chocolate brownies was enough to make me want to become a baker. Or a chef. Or whatever it is you're called when you can make chocolate brownies. Marmite has the edge for me but chocolate brownies are heavenly and you can get all the ingredients in one go from 1-800-555-1701. I was just wondering how much I could make and how long they would last, then I was smiling at the idea of there being a best-before date when I was surely going to

eat every last one IMMEDIATELY, and that's when I saw the blue elephant.

I don't mean that he was morose, I mean he was an elephant and he appeared to be blue. There was a screaming, roaring, bellowing sound from his trunk as he zoomed by me at the closest to light-speed that modern physics and four feet can manage. No sooner had I realised he was charging at me then he was gone, my OXO cube sandwich snatched out of my hand and my red face matching the Doppler-shifted elephant as it ran away at about 0.9c.

And here are the answers:

Marmite
I didn't give you my number
The elephant is grey

It's not true about Marmite, to be fair and in case we ever meet for lunch, but it is true that the elephant is grey because elephants always are. I told you this was called the Red Elephant Experiment so that you would notice that I then said that the beast was blue.

You'll notice that actually I was careful to say that the elephant appeared to be blue. I played with the notion that it was just an upset kind of elephant, but then told you the elephant was red – and said that this was because of the Doppler effect.

If you don't happen to know what that is then, bugger. It's like when you hear a car coming toward you and then going away; that rising sound and then falling sound, it's called the Doppler effect and it happens with light, too, especially when you're moving really, really fast. An object coming toward you that fast, getting on for c, the speed of light, will look blue and then when it's gone by, when it's travelling away at that same speed, it'll look red. But it's still a grey elephant.

You know that I'm hoping something of all this surprised you. That I'm hoping you somehow failed to spot something, anything, in that passage and that I can therefore now say multitasking clobbers your comprehension of a passage. You are exactly right. That is exactly my point.

Except... one more thing.

Was that passage any good?

I'll save you the trouble of going back up to read it again and tell you that no, it was a piece of rubbish written out in less time and with less effort than it took you to read it. But because you were going in looking for those three answers, you weren't going in with even the possibility of enjoyment. I'm glad because you'd have been let down if you had, but this is what's really important, this is what means multitasking doesn't just slow you down.

You're a writer, you know this: writing is not about facts and lightspeed and brownies, it is about feeling and emotion and people. It's about conveying far more than is specifically, literally written on the page. If it weren't, it wouldn't be so bloody hard to do.

Let us agree, then, that multitasking does not help you get two things done at the same time – and that trying it blinds you to the value and the worth of what you're doing.

If you take only one thing away from this entire book, I am rubbish and you were robbed. But make it be this one about multitasking:

> Do one thing at a time.
>
> Finish the chapter, the scene, the email, the washing, the cooking.

I know that's not practical. You're going to get interrupted, you're going to have to stop to think about what you're writing next, something urgent is going to come up. There is always the issue of what's the most important thing, what is a priority right now. I can't take away much of this but I can reduce it – especially the idea of priorities – and I can tell you, I can stress and underline, that even trying to finish the one thing will help you.

Recently I was trying to explain to someone why I was ignoring a particular script note from my editor. He's a smart editor, it was a good point and I wasn't precious about making the change, but of all the things he said, I was choosing to ignore that one because I knew something better. The way I eventually summarised it was that if the final script is great, nobody cares whether you followed the notes or not. If the script is bad, no audience will give you a gold star for having diligently addressed every note.

It's the same thing here. If you get something done, done well and fast enough or just soon enough that it was still useful, nobody cares that you didn't drop everything else and start on it right away.

That bit about doing it fast enough or soon enough is key, though. It's all about priorities and that's the second issue we need to deal with.

Chapter 2

Altered priorities ahead

I found this one a doddle. I don't know why. It just seemed to fit very naturally with the way my mind works or the methods I was starting to do to get on top of all the work. Giving up multitasking was tough, learning a new approach to priorities was effortless.

That's nice for me, isn't it? I just want to underline for you that some productivity things you'll get straight away, some you won't. And of those some that you won't, there are ones where you should ignore them because they'll never work for you and there are others where you should at least try because they're key and important. The ones in these first chapters are most definitely both.

It is definitely, certainly the case that you need to work on priorities. And I think it's especially so because businesses expect you to be able to do prioritise and most To Do software goes on at you about how brilliant they are at it. You can number your tasks in priority order, you can give them star ratings, you can tag them as vital or trivial, there are endless ways to make your To Do list multi-coloured.

We're going to talk about To Do lists a lot but before we get into more paper, I need to say this to you right now:

> If your phone can have a To Do app, get a To Do app

And:

> If your phone can't have a To Do app, get a phone that can.

Sometimes I'm going to sound as if I'm knocking To Do software, especially when I ask you to get paper, but my position is just about completely the other way around. Very soon now, you're going to see your list as something useful instead of something to avoid but if it isn't in software and it isn't with you constantly, you might as well not have one. You'll see why it's nowhere conceivably good enough to rely on Post-It notes but for a sneak peek ahead at one gigantic reason why, take a peek back at the phrase 'Post-It notes'. Notes. Plural. You won't have just the one. You won't. So now which list is up to date, which has all the tasks on it, which hasn't, where did you leave them? Yeah. Good luck with that.

Mind you, having dissed pen and paper, I'm afraid I actually need you to hang on to your Biro for just a little bit more.

And I need you to please write out the following list of tasks for me in priority order. Number them. Which you think is priority 1, which is priority 2, and so on. There's no stopwatch on you for this, you can do it as carefully and slowly or as fast and casual as you like. Just pretend that this is a real list, that it's your real list, and then do it the way you would in real life.

Get aspirin 1
Reply to Tom 2
Buy broccoli 5
Research chapter 3 4
Phone re mistake on bill 3
Read Pride and Prejudice 6

Are you done?

You've now got a list of six items and they are ranked in order from 1 to 6. Unfortunately, the phone just rang and your boss/editor/producer/biggest client needs you to write a report justifying what you've been doing or they won't pay you this month.

That's changed your list, hasn't it? You'd have to have a steady hand to have just added your boss to the list as number 7. I would also point out that you're a bit lucky if you've left enough room at the top of the page to fit that task in. And when you get a second demand from that boss, a second emergency, a third imperative task, there isn't enough luck in the world and you'll be writing out the whole list again on another page.

But regardless of how many times you have to write this thing, if that boss task is now easily and obviously number 1, what's the seventh and least? You could say "read Pride and Prejudice" but then you don't know what a great book it is, you're off my Christmas card list – and you're probably not just about to interview Jane Austen. Okay, so you go for broccoli as that clearly isn't important – but if the shop's closing in five minutes, suddenly it's urgent and you'd better go for it in another sense.

There's a lovely sequence about this in the BBC television series *Yes, Prime Minister* by Antony Jay and Jonathan Lynn. The show is famous but what's less well-known is that they later adapted it into a book of what was purportedly the edited and annotated political diaries of its lead character, Jim Hacker, MP who writes:

I was wading through some Cabinet Defence Papers in the office this morning when Bernard interrupted me.

"Excuse me, Minister, but I'm afraid you have to deal with something that is much more urgent."

I asked what.

"Your Christmas cards, Minister. They cannot be postponed any longer."

Bernard was right. Getting the Christmas cards out is much more important than reading Cabinet Defence Papers – unless you're the Secretary of State for Defence, I suppose.

[Hacker, like many politicians, was apparently unable to distinguish between 'Urgent' and 'Important'. Bernard had described the Christmas cards as the former. Hacker assumed that he meant the latter – Ed.]

(Yes, Prime Minister: The Diaries of the Right Hon. James Hacker, vol 1. Edited by Jonathan Lynn and Antony Jay, BBC Publications 1986)

There's a good argument that this priority exercise is impossible anyway. Or at least pretty impossible without more information about each of the tasks on it. For all you know, Tom has just texted to say that he loves you and is going to do something drastic if you don't reply in kind and quickly. Maybe the aspirin isn't for you but for a gunman who's taken hostages and is demanding the pills plus a plane to Cuba. There's a really good argument that you always need more information and that you always need more context before you prioritise. It is true.

But actually it's no help. It is always more useful to have a task called "Reply to Tom re lovelorn leap off lover's lane bridge" than just "Reply to Tom" but there is always more information, there is always more context – and even a finely-tuned and usefully-detailed list of priorities will always be shattered by the boss phoning.

So how did I rank those? I didn't.

I didn't prioritise them at all. Instead, while you were numbering them, I got some aspirin and I texted Tom to say I'm flattered but I'm married, didn't he read the introduction? Also, try not to enter the water at an angle, it just prolongs things.

I'm a smartarse, yes, but now I've just got five things left to do where you still have seven.

If something is a big number 1, five-star, underlined, red-coloured priority, you would have done it before you even put it on your list. That's not to say that everything on your list is equally important or equally trivial, it is to say that you shouldn't spend your limited time sweating details to fit your To Do app's priority features. It isn't necessary, it does not help and the time you have to spend studying your To Do list app is time you could be using to get this stuff done.

There's a particularly smart and entertaining speaker named Merlin Mann who must be particularly smart because he thinks the same way as I do on this issue. He just says it considerably more effectively:

> Got news for you, Jack: if it moves, it's not a priority. It's just a thing you haven't done yet.
>
> Making something a BIG RED TOP TOP BIG HIGHEST #1 PRIORITY changes nothing but text styling. If it were really important, it'd already be done. Period. Think about it.
>
> Example. When my daughter falls down and screams, I don't ask her to wait while I grab a list to determine which of seven notional levels of "priority" I should assign to her need for instantaneous care and affection. Everything stops, and she gets taken care of.
>
> Conversely -- and this is really the important part -- everything else in the universe can wait.
>
> Related example. You ever had a loved one -- especially a very young relative -- pass away unexpectedly? Brutal. What did you do

> when you found out? Did you "re-prioritize" your day and move a few things around? Or did you drop everything and join his or her loved ones in taking care of what needed to be taken care of? You just saw what needed to be done and likely had no compunction about telling everybody at work they'd either have to wait or move on without you.
>
> And, let's be clear: this is not all about "urgency." Yes, an injured child and a grieving family need help now in a way that an M&A discussion or a CPR class may not. But, again. It's not a question of order or shuffling. It's a question of brutally honest decision-making and constantly saying, "No, I have another thing to take care of."
>
> Day One Buddhism.
>
> Because, once you see what's really there -- once you know about an idea or a thing or a person or whatever that you'd reject 10,000 other things to protect and nurture -- you've found your priority. And, consequently, you've discovered a bunch of other things that aren't allowed to be priorities any more. Even in spirit.
>
> Because, if you aren't rejecting or dumping things every single day, you don't know your priority. You're making things up. If you think you have 35 priorities, then yes: you also think you have 35 arms. Is it any wonder you're feeling awkward and unsure?
>
> *(Merlin Mann, 43Folders, 2009)*

Take a look at that site, 43Folders.com: Mann doesn't update it now but there's a lot to enjoy, including that priorities essay. He runs a podcast called *Back to Work* – I'm not keen on its zoo format where the hosts are having a better time than the listeners but people who like it, like it a lot. But he crops up on *Mac Power Users* which I am addicted to.

So:

> Don't piddle about prioritising the perfect To Do list, get on with what you have to do.

And do it one thing at a time.

All of which is great and I do really mean that all of it is useful, but it doesn't help when you've got a To Do list fifteen miles long.

That's what my third thing is all about.

Chapter 3

Taken to task

You can't multitask and you shouldn't prioritise so plainly I'm going to tell you now that you shouldn't write To Do lists.

Yes. Pretty much. Or at least that you shouldn't write them the way you do now. For there are specific things we all tend to do on our lists that rather guarantee they'll be useless when we come to work through the list after lunch.

But there are also issues here that are more kind of philosophical/conceptual (delete whichever term irritates you the most). And when we get those in our heads, we can do our lists much better.

There is the small thing that having a gigantic To Do list may be precisely what is stopping you writing anything at all. There's the little matter that having to keep referring to a list sounds like madness.

So let's just fix those two things.

We can do so much better than ordinary To Do lists. We can make To Do lists be useful, we can even make them be fantastically useful. And I know, I actually have seen that getting this point into your head changes you. This is the bit where I felt lighter. But only eventually, only after I understood it.

So let's see how well I understood it by seeing how well I can show you what I've found along the way.

First of all, this is what normal people think a To Do list is:

> A list of things you need to do. You do it and you cross off the done stuff. Then you go on to the next thing.

And this is what the untrained eye who read the last chapter would call a To Do list:

> Get aspirin
> Reply to Tom
> Buy broccoli
> Research chapter 3
> Phone re mistake on bill
> Read Pride and Prejudice

You now know all about not bothering to sort that list into some convoluted sequence of priorities, you know to just get on with it. So let's say you get on with it and you do exactly what everybody in the world believes you do with a To Do list. Item 1: get aspirin. The only trouble is, it's now 2am and there are no pharmacies, no garages and no chance you've got any left in the bathroom cabinet.

If we really worked To Do lists the way people think, if we could work them that way and were literal kinds of people, we'd now stop. Can't get aspirin, therefore can't tick it off the list, therefore can't go on to the next thing. The end. You're shrugging now. You're definitely thinking that you'd just move on to the next thing and maybe you're also thinking that about the only idea less obvious in this world is that night follows day. So without thinking, you'd move on and start replying to Tom.

But look at exactly what you've just done. You've ignored the sequence, you've rejected the first thing To Do and you have decided that it Can't Be Done Yet. All I want you to do is to look at the entire list in much that same way – with maybe one twiddle.

In fact, rather than looking at the aspirin and deciding it Can't Be Done Yet, the one twiddle is that you need to look at the Reply to Tom one instead and call that a task that Can Be Done Now.

That little list I wrote there is rubbish for a lot of reasons which we'll go through in the detailed next section on To Do lists, but better than anything you can do to the list is what you can do to your head. To Do lists are not lists of things to do. They are lists of things you can do.

It sounds obvious or it sounds really silly: it doesn't sound like common sense. But it's important because when you see this the old way, as lists of things you've got to do, you are also seeing that you haven't done any of them yet. More, you cannot help but unconsciously regard the list as a failure. Even with the aspirin: that trivial gun-siege aspirin: you need some, you want some, you can't have it, therefore you're a failure.

I don't believe in excusing failure or blaming the parents – if it's the fault of our parents that we've turned out the way we have, are their own failings therefore the fault of their own parents? And their parents one generation back? I understand wanting to duck blame but how far back are you willing to go with this cover-up? I believe that failure is an option and that without it we can't spot when we succeed. But in this case, there's no parental lawsuit, there's nothing of any great significance or importance but every time you look at your list and see what you haven't done, you think you've failed. And you're genuinely, blamelessly wrong.

But wrong or right, trivial or significant, you saw the aspirin as a failure and then you looked at Tom. Let's say you did that task. You replied to Tom, sorted him out, all's good now and you come back to the list to tick that off. Terrific. But now your list reads:

Get aspirin
~~Reply to Tom~~
Buy broccoli
Research chapter 3
Phone re mistake on bill
Read Pride and Prejudice

If you do this on paper and you cross out each one you've done, you do undeniably get an increasing satisfaction at seeing more and more crossed out. But if you do your list on a computer, once it's done, it's gone. Tap that checkbox and your list immediately shrinks to:

Get aspirin
Buy broccoli
Research chapter 3
Phone re mistake on bill
Read Pride and Prejudice

But at least it's shrinking and that is good, right? It is and it is. Except when did your To Do list last shrink? Usually you're adding to it and usually you're adding many other tasks forever. Unfortunately you're also usually doing some things over and over again. I have a recurring To Do to remind me I have to put the bins out on Wednesday mornings. Tick. That task is gone from my list – but, no, there it is, right back there again, waiting for next Wednesday.

For now, say the list doesn't repeat and you don't add anything else to it, it has just shrunk to those five. You pick the list up again and the first thing you are going to do is read 'Get aspirin' because it's right there, it's top of the list. And it's only two minutes since you last looked so you still can't get the pills so you're still failing. It's 2:02am and the supermarket isn't open either so nuts to your need to 'Buy broccoli'. You've had nights where you've thought about all the things you've got to do and they were all a sight more important than vegetables and pills. But few of them could be done at that time of night so actually they are all the same, they all scream at you that they're important yet you can't do them then.

Our lists get clogged up with things that, yes, are very important, are perhaps very urgent, but we physically cannot do them right this second. So it's water torture seeing these items on the list and the typical To Do list is a constant, continual, never-ending lists of things you can't do.

Much worse, I think, is that you have to rethink and reevaluate every single thing on the list, pretty much every single time you look at it. When I see my Wednesday bin task, for instance, I'm afraid that there is one half of one moment where I'm thinking "Is that this Wednesday or next? Have I done this week's or not? Can I do something else or can I relax?" Every time. Even with the aspirin, for one pixel of a second, you read that and you are thinking about whether you can get some now.

Computers help. Apps help. They also hinder. We don't tend to put dates on our To Do lists when we're writing them on paper, but in software we do. So you know that I would put the bins task in with a date of the coming Wednesday and when that day came around, that task might well change to red. Or I'll get an alarm for it late on Tuesday night.

Shrug.

Doesn't matter. I'll still be scrolling through my To Do list throughout the week and I'll still see the bins task every time I do. Of course I'll know I haven't had an alarm and perhaps I'll see that it hasn't yet changed red, but I will look and I will know and I will see every single time.

Except when I need to. Forget aspirin and bins, think about that "Phone re mistake on bill". That's clearly very important, that's clearly an urgent priority and I can understand wanting to see that every single time. But now it's 2:04am – you're having a bad night – and whichever company sent you the bill doesn't have a 24-hour weep line. Fine, so you can't do it then. But then tomorrow at work, you look at your list and think, bugger, that's got to be done right now – and the bill's back at home on your kitchen table.

Over and over it goes. We are constantly working at our To Do lists and

I'm fine with working and I am here to work, but we should be working at what we've got to do, not at the list of it.

Acceptance

The first step in that is to accept that you are not going to get everything done. Not today. All those things you put on your list because they were important, most of them are going to be there tomorrow. That's yet another reason why To Do lists make you miserable: we can't do them all so we don't do any. But if you take away the churning, constant re-evaluation of every task and you change it to a Can Be Done list, you will get more done.

Just not everything. It's so hard to accept that this is okay, but it honestly is. I promise.

Think about this. You usually put something on your To Do list for tomorrow because it is important and tomorrow is the first day you can do it. You don't tend to put it there because it is actually due tomorrow or because someone is specifically relying on you to do it tomorrow. Yet because there it is on your list the next morning, you think it has to be done and you feel awful when you simply can't get to it.

Routinely, the last thing you'll do in the day is work over the whole bleedin' list yet again and this time go through marking various tasks saying they must be done tomorrow. And tomorrow and tomorrow and tomorrow.

Your job is not to put the task on your list, it is to get the task done.

So, okay, maybe you get that putting everything straight down on a list is the way to misery. You could work very hard at your whole list and assign tasks to days. Bins are Wednesday, phoning about that bill really does have to be tomorrow, and reading Pride & Prejudice can wait until Saturday at 9am. You could do this and it would help, but there's more and there is better. Much better.

Seriously: it's not To Do, it's Can Be Done

You have to do this in software. Some people like the *Getting Things Done* productivity guru David Allen say you can do it all on paper but I mustn't be as clever as him because I haven't a clue how you'd start. Particularly because the first job is hide tasks. Well, first you write them, but then you hide them from yourself.

Because unless it's something actually, genuinely due today, I don't want to keep seeing it every time I look at my list.

So write down your tasks in your To Do list software of choice but only give them a time, a deadline, when they genuinely have one. Otherwise, let them be hidden away completely. You're going to have to bear with me on this one, I can tell. But hang on in there.

If you've got to deliver a script to a director on the 1st, put that in. If, instead, you've got to get it to the director when it's done, don't put any date at all. Just put down "Email script to director when ready" and nothing else. It sounds like you're writing the task down but don't really mean to do it. And if this weren't in software, it would be exactly like writing down a long list and seeing it all every time.

But because it's software, we can put a task in and not have to look at it until we need to. I have to tell you that some software helps in this line, some does not. It's very variable. But they all do something with dates so whatever phone or tablet app or computer software you have, you can get something of this effect at least.

The ideal situation is for your software to not force you to set a date at all. Just let you enter the task. The only slightly less ideal is for your software to do the opposite, to insist on dates but to let you set not just a deadline date but also a first date you can look at something. A start date. I had a gig once where I was spending a month interviewing various people for a particular project but I got the job about two weeks beforehand. So I put it in, I put the ultimate end-of-next-month deadline, but I also set a start date. And until the month began, I didn't have those ten interviews clogging up my To Do list. I didn't have them at all: they simply got hidden away until I needed them.

They were hidden away because I didn't need to see them until the first of the month. Other tasks are hidden away because I don't want to see them at all. That's actually a bit scary at first. Strike that, it's very scary.

You're putting a task in your To Do list and then it's immediately gone. Vanished. You understand, intellectually, that you don't want to see about the bins until next Tuesday night at the earliest, but sitting there in the pub on Saturday, waiting for someone and trying to look busily cool, you wonder if that task has actually been lost forever.

You'll wonder if you ever entered it. The quick answer to that one is that if you think of a task and you aren't sure if you entered it, don't go doubting your mind, your sanity or your To Do app. Just add it again. Why not? Come Tuesday night, if my To Do app tells me to empty the bins twice, that's better than it not telling me at all.

The trick of hiding the tasks away is that you choose when to see them. They're not there in your face every single time you look at your list. They appear when you've told them to – or when you go looking for them. And you go looking at them because periodically you review your entire list. You do that bit of seeing every item but you do it when you decided to.

You're not convinced. But there's more in the detailed To Do section that follows this, the one that says what to press when and that won't convince you either. You'll only be convinced when you've done this for yourself and for some time. But while I want to steadily nudge you this way, the quick headline explanation for its success is that you will review the list often enough that you don't miss anything – and not so often that you can't bear looking at the list at all.

I just looked into my own list and I've seen that I have a task called "Buy Shoes". It has no start date, it has no deadline, it does not appear on my daily list of tasks. But even if I hadn't just peeked, I'd have seen that when I did my regular review tomorrow. So for the moment the task is out of my head but I'll see it tomorrow. And then I'll see it on Friday, which happens to be when my next regular review is. So I don't lose the task, I don't forget it, I just don't have to carry it on my daily list or in my head.

If you put "Buy Shoes" on your regular To Do list you would see it every day until you did it. You would see it many times a day, exactly as many times as you looked at your list. But you still won't do it until you're near a shoe shop, you still won't do it any faster for it being in your face. So there is a difference to having it there or hidden, there is a difference between catching it on your next review or every night moving it on to tomorrow's list. But the differences are all bad. None of them are good. The differences get in your way and they don't get you the shoes any sooner.

You just have to trust yourself that you'll catch the task in your next review or the one after, or the one after that. And – this may be the hardest part – you have to trust that your To Do app will show you the task when you want to see it.

Guru David Allen talks a lot about a "trusted system" and he's absolutely right. I completely trust that OmniFocus for iPhone will take anything I lob at it while I run around all day and that it will immediately put those new tasks on my iPad and on my Mac. I reach for the nearest screen, whichever device it is, and I add another task or I do another task.

Trust your To Do app. You're great at doing tasks, your To Do app is designed to remember that you need to do them. Plus – no, okay, let me give you a real-life example of what happens when you don't trust your To Do list. Or perhaps when you don't trust yourself to look at your list.

A friend of mine has this thing he has to do every day. I think it's about 4pm every day, something like that. It's important. So he puts it in his To Do list but it's so important that he worries he will forget to look at the list in time each day. Naturally, then, he sets an alert, an alarm on the task.

Only, this thing has to be done at 4pm and he sets an alarm for something like 7am. Maybe 8am. It's set to go off over breakfast and before he leaves for work. I get that: he has to bring something or get something or do something so that he can be ready to do this thing at 4pm in his schedule.

But he also sets an alarm for 10am to remind him that it's going to happen this afternoon. Sometimes he's going to have meetings and he'll know what those are by 10am so he's effectively reminded less to do this thing, more to arrange his time so that he can.

He also sets an alarm for 11am. And for noon. There's one more for over lunch and then there's one at 3pm that says it's an hour to the thing.

And finally, at 4pm, his iPhone pops up with the reminder:

> Take your stress pill

If something works for you, do it. But I would offer that at the very most, the only alarms my friend benefits from are the first two and the last. For the first, he knows to pack his pills. For the second, this is more of a stretch, he knows to check his calendar for the afternoon. Other than that, the 11am, noon, lunch and 3pm ones are useless because he cannot use them. There is nothing to be done when those reminders go off.

So at least four of his seven alarms for this task are only there to interrupt whatever else he's doing through the day. I suggest that they also encourage the worry that he'll miss the 4pm one. They're there to help but they end up contributing to the stress, in my opinion.

Trust your system to remind you and trust yourself to hear its alarms and reminders. This is easier for men than women. Seriously. It's like nearly every man's shirt has been designed for a phone and every woman's handbag is built to ray-shield the sound of ringing. Phones can all be turned up high enough to be heard through handbags but I'm not sure a choice between missing an alarm or opening your bag and being deafened is really an actual choice.

I seem to be assuming you do or you will use your phone for To Do reminders and maybe that's just a function of how wedded I am to mine. You can get the same thing on tablets; that might suit you better. But whatever it is, however you use it, trust that the way it worked reminding you today is the way it will remind you tomorrow and forever.

It does take a long time to build up trust and to build up your reliance on software and any problem like data corruption or the smallest data loss means that trust is gone.

But you will get that trust back if your software is good enough. Unfortunately, finding one that is good is hard because we can trade specifications and prices all we want, the goodness of something in software is much less tangible.

Still, do make sure that you know how your software deals with all this – check if it has Start Dates for instance – and then surrender to it. I wrote about OmniFocus in a magazine once and said something like "First it destroys your mind, then it owns your soul." That was a five-star Editor's Choice recommended pick. So I meant it as a compliment.

It's funny but for a category of software that seems very obviously all the same sort of thing, there is tremendous variety. I just had a look on both the Google Play Store for Android and the Apple App Store for iOS and they both have in excess of eleventy-billion To Do apps. Look at the chapter on Making Your Computer Work Harder for You to get an idea of how in the world you find the right one for you but I'll tell you now that the best tip is to try any of the free ones first. Just see what they do and whether they're at all right for you. Then you'll know enough of what you like and don't like to understand what people are going on about in reviews.

Free probably means basic but it needn't mean rubbish. Macs and iPhones come with Apple's Reminders which while it isn't great for running your life, it did bring us location reminders. Every decent To Do app has been racing to add that same feature ever since and the best ones have got it and are consequently just as fantastic. The ability to be reminded of something not on a given day but the next time you go somewhere. Or just when you leave here. It's startling at first and then much more startling to think there was ever a time when we didn't have it.

But that's all getting too specific. That's all starting to talk about press-this-button, say-that-thing. And that's what we're going to cover next: how to write your To Do list regardless of what software you use.

If you're now wondering whether I'm about to tell you some better way to write down the words "Call Dad" then yes. You bet your life I am.

Chapter 4

What to do

The last chapter was philosophical about one's ultimate perception of To Do lists. This one is the complete opposite: it is about precisely what you need to do, how you need to do it and I even throw in when. It's picky and all of it is a question of using really small steps or making really tiny changes to how you work, but that's one thing that is good about it: with just the teeniest effort you can get great rewards.

And the chief great reward is time. There's no question but that it is very satisfying to tick off one thing as done and that it is immeasurably satisfying to look at a whole list and tick a dozen things at once. But the chief reward and the overall aim is to get you to the stage where you can spend less time on the To Dos and more time on your writing.

So it might seem a bit wrong to start by saying that you need to spend more time on writing your To Do tasks.

If you take one thing away from this section, make it this:

> Always write your To Do tasks as if they are going to be done by someone else.

You get the idea and you can see that it will take longer, but let's be specific. Instead of writing "Reply to Tom", you need to write something like "Reply to Tom about spurning his advances". Instead of "Buy broccoli" write "Buy tender stem broccoli."

When you do this, when you're writing that down, it seems a waste of time. It would be much more efficient to write a list named "Calls" and just put Tom's name on it. And "Shopping" with broccoli. It would definitely be faster, I'll agree with you there. But I've got a quiet day tomorrow, for example, and I only need to phone five people so my Calls list would be:

> Naomi
> Peter
> Eric
> Janet
> Acme Publishing Co

I made that last name up but I do need to call a particular publisher. Instead of just listing those names, though, I've written this:

> Phone Naomi to arrange a coffee re NYC
> Phone Peter to discuss standing order bank details
> Phone Eric re boiler repair estimates
> Ring Janet to see how she is after the op
> Phone Acme Publishing Co to find out imprint editor's name and email

I have no idea why I wrote "Ring" for Janet instead of "Phone". I probably dictated it into Siri on my iPhone so maybe I say ring more often than I write it. But however I did it, typing or dictating, you know that it took longer to do a list this way rather than just writing down the names. The few extra seconds that took, though, will save me vastly more time later.

I find my most successful phone calls are made between 11am and 12noon – that may just be a function of who I ring but it works so I stick to it – and I will do it from that list. Fire up the list, see I need to ring Naomi about a New York City project. (New York is my favourite place in the world and I will talk to anyone about anything to do with it. Especially over coffee.) Then I'll phone Peter and I'll phone Eric and it all goes on and on. You can see that each time I hang up from one person, I can be dialling the next knowing precisely what I need to talk to them about.

Of course you don't get everybody and of course they don't then phone back when they say they will – there's not much you can do about that but the chapter on *The Curse of Other People* tells you some – but I'll make those five calls in a row, bang, bang, bang. I haven't worked out an average number of calls I do or even attempted to measure the typical times but I'd be surprised if I weren't back to writing by 11:30am.

So that's where the time saving is. You spend a little extra time when you're writing your task and you save much more when you come to do it. I said you should write your tasks as if someone else is going to do them and really, someone else is. The you who writes the list tonight is not quite the same person as the you who is doing the task tomorrow. Even normal people will have thought a million thoughts in between writing the list and doing it; how much more lost in your work do you get when you're writing? And then how much more lost do you get when you're writing to a deadline?

There are limits to this but in general the more you can do up front when you're making the list, the less you have to do when you're actually doing the task.

Enough already

You need to find out how much detail in a To Do list is just too much detail for you. Let me show you what I'd call impossible overkill:

> Task: Send invoice for Coca Cola feature to Al Phabet at Acme Publishing Co.
> Type of Task: Email
> Start date: Thursday
> Start time: 9:00am
> Due date: Thursday
> Due time: 9:30am
> Project: Money
> Estimated duration: 5 minutes
> Repeat: never
> Energy Level Required: Low
> Flagged: on
> Notes: {attached Word document with feature copy and fee agreement}

Be honest: not only would you never write all that, you didn't even read it. I barely read it.

The task itself is fine: I doubt I'd say both Al Phabet and Acme Publishing; all I really need in order to know what to do is that it's an invoice, what it's for and who it's to. So it'd be one or other. The fact that I say which feature it was for might be enough too.

If you're thinking that's all you'd do, excellent. If you're thinking that actually, you wouldn't even schedule this as a To Do task, you'd just do the invoice then you are more excellent still and my accountant wishes I were as good as you.

Only, whether you're a minimalist like me or you love the precision of, say, being able to look up every task that will take you less than ten minutes, the truth is that you won't be consistent. And you shouldn't be. There's no need to be. Always and forever, you must write the task as if it's going to be done by someone else but the rest is up for grabs. Hand on heart, I have never and I will never put in an estimated duration and I can't conceive of taking the time to think whether I'll need lots or little energy in order to pull them off. Many To Do apps let you do this – and I've just looked, the one I use does the time one – but I won't ever use it.

Then flags, which I believe all To Do software has, are just another way of marking something as being high priority and I did try it: I intend to watch a friend's video online and I flagged it four months ago. I'm flagging, but not in the sense you'd want.

But I will almost always assign a task to a project. As I run around town or making the arduous commute up and down the stairs to my kitchen, I will be add new tasks to my To Do list and they'll be clear though they'll be basic. Then very, very often I work over that list just to add a little detail. Nearly always, I'll say that this particular task is to do with my general Money project, this is for Acme Publishing, that's for the Writer's Guild. Doing that means these tasks don't sit there on my big daily list, they're tucked away off in a list for the Guild or wherever.

Just adding that information tucks them away neatly and that's nice but the true benefit to me is that it gets them out of my head. And it also lets me choose when to load them all back in there in one convenient go. For instance, the next time I want to do something with Acme Publishing – say I'm going to their office – I can look at the Acme project and see everything I've got to do with them. Every idea I've had, every task I've agreed to, the lot. If an Acme editor phones me out of the blue and asks how things are going then, well, frankly they're going to regret it because I know. I know in detail. That freaks people out. It's great.

I can't do that without some effort, it's just that because I'm always on the case, I don't have to make the effort when the phone rings. I suppose there's a certain element of self-discipline in all this but I promise you it's a very small element. I'm the laziest man you'll ever meet but I have help: the To Do software I use nudges me into being more efficient. It nudges me so gently that I am completely nudged. For when you're using this OmniFocus, your new tasks sit there in one big inbox until you do something about it. Just a little something. Tap the task and add that it's part of your project on Taking Over the World. That's all.

I do that and the task bounds off out of the inbox and goes and plays in the Taking Over the World list. That one little thing means I don't have to see that task until the next time I choose to look up that project or unless I've added some dates to it.

Throwing countless tasks into my inbox all day is fantastic: it means I can capture the smallest stray thought and know that it'll be there for me to work on later. But then clearing the inbox is essential. Because that inbox can pile up like mad over my typical day and when I leave things in there, it feels like I haven't got a handle on them. But that may just be me.

Speaking of me, I quite often mark a task as being a phone call. It's usually very obvious just from the task name but if I also mark it as being one, then later when I'm waiting for a train I can choose to look up all the calls I need to make and start knocking them off. It's much the same with emails. If my calls run on and I don't finish until, say, 11:50am, then I will often just look at the list of emails I have to do and fire off a couple of those rather than start back with my writing until the top of the hour. It doesn't matter to me that this email is to do with Acme Publishing and that next email is to do with a favour I promised a friend. I just see a list of emails and each task is clear enough that I can go straight to writing.

I'm happy with marking tasks as being phone or email, I'm dead set on really clear task names, but I'm trying to wean myself off setting start dates. I over-use them. It is truly much better not to have any dates at all and just trust that your To Do app will remember them, to trust that you will see them when you regularly review all of your list. But I do successfully resist putting in due dates unless it's a genuine deadline.

The point of all this, though, is that your mileage varies and the proof is that mine already does. That's the way that it should be. The job is to get this task done as easily and quickly as possible. If only every task was a single thing you could get done between 11am and 11:30am.

It's more complicated than that

I did actually put "Write productivity book" into my To Do list. It was a ridiculous task to put in because it's just too big and also there's no obvious time to tick it off as completed: I could say it was done when I started the book – since I'm doing it, I will never need that task to prompt me again – or I could do it when the book is finished and published. I could wait until you started reading it.

More, it's an unhelpful To Do because it doesn't give me enough information. It is clear, yet it's not clear in any useful way. You can't and I didn't look at that and go straight to the keyboard.

However, it did its job. The fact that you're reading this says that but really its job was not to get me to write this to you, it was to get me to think about the project. Perhaps I should've made the task be "Plan productivity book". That is better but at the time, once again driving somewhere and telling Siri to remember this thought, I wasn't finished thinking about whether to do it or not. I threw it into my To Do list to make sure I'd got it down, then I could think about it later. I would think about it quite soon, but not that very moment.

Next chance I got, I looked at all the tasks I'd thrown in via Siri. Some I'd actually done where I was driving to, so those got ticked off immediately. The rest got parcelled off into projects and I think there was at least one that I knew had a genuine deadline, so I added that. Then I got to the "Write productivity book" one and I thought about it more.

I wanted to do this book, no question. I wanted to talk to you and I knew there was all this stuff that had so incredibly helped me, I wanted it all to help you. But I am a freelance writer and like all of us, my only stock is time. There is a physical limit to how much we can do and though I test that, though I've improved it for myself and I hope to improve it for you, there is still the issue of there being only 168 hours in a week and we all have commitments.

Full disclosure: the wanting to write this to you actually won out over the practicalities of time. I know you cannot care how I choose to spend my week and that it's very big of me to say I decided to write to you, but don't forget the wanting. In all this productivity lark, you can get so focused on turning over work quickly, getting to the next task, finishing the job and getting the next one, that you forget we like writing. Being productive will give us more time for our writing, we ought to spend some of that on writing what we want.

So hello. Very nice to see you. And I'm here with *The Blank Screen* because once I decided to do this, I deleted that "Write productivity book" task.

I didn't mark it as done. I deleted it. And started planning. The task had done its job and I'd begun working: I began working by figuring out what my next tasks are.

The next task or "next action" is a particularly key part of David Allen's *Getting Things Done* book that I've now mentioned three times. There's more about it in the *Stolen Goods* chapter but the headline is that is a very clever productivity book that is peculiarly dated and wasn't aimed at us writers anyway. Nonetheless, I use a lot of its ideas and so does writer/director Joss Whedon. He has a reputation for tremendous productivity – he took a fortnight off at the end of filming one movie and made another, start to finish, before going back to edit the first one – and he advocates this "next action" mantra. He got it from David Allen, too, even though he says never managed to finish reading *Getting Things Done*:

> I told him, actually, because he did a little talk at someone's house and I did tell him, "You should write a second book called Finishing This Book.' But it has been enormously helpful, even in the baby steps version that I embrace. I still use the phrases 'Next actions' is one of the most important things that you can say in any endeavor.

Quick aside? I used to write for *Radio Times* a lot and I remember around 2004 having a couple of DVDs to watch for them. It was a very unusual situation where the DVDs came in a couple of months before the show was due to air so I could leave those discs on my desk and I did because it was just *Battlestar Galactica*. It was a remake of a 1970s failed show, it was going to end up on Sky's movie channel rather than primetime Sky One (originally anyway) and there was a lot of new, high-profile, major UK dramas launching at that time. Weeks go by until one night, with nothing else to do and a regular long trip ahead of me, I took one of those two discs. And by the end of my trip I was hopping mad that I hadn't brought the second as well. It is utterly riveting human drama, completely compelling.

To this day, there's a throwaway line from an especially strong episode – *33* by Ronald D Moore – that I keep using.

Here's the moment from that script. You need to know that there were

50,000 survivors of the most gigantic apocalypse and that now something else, something very bad has just happened. It's happened and there is nothing anyone can do that can make it any better. Now read on:

```
INT. COLONIAL ONE - OFFICE

Laura watches Billy update the board --
47,972. She stares at the number, tries
not to let it get to her, but the burden
is there nonetheless. REVEAL Baltar sit-
ting nearby.

Finally, Laura is ready to move on.

                    LAURA
          Okay. Next crisis?
```

That's it. The phrase "Next crisis". I don't know why that sticks with me and it feels very cheapening to think that someone in the midst of that level of drama and tragedy would stop to read *Getting Things Done*. But oftentimes, I'll finish a big sequence of tasks and I will say – I will say aloud – "Next crisis?"

The key there, I think, is that I do it after a big sequence of tasks and before beginning the next big sequence. Very few things you ever do are single tasks that are complete and on their own. "Buy broccoli" may be the only one. Even then, maybe you even have an entire recipe to follow and a big shopping list. But as tasks go, it's on the small side.

For everything else, it's fine to start with "Write productivity book" but as soon as you can, delete that and begin writing what the real tasks are. Specifically what the real next task is, the next action, the next crisis.

Next tasks

Let's call any big sequence of tasks a project. That's what the To Do software I use calls them, that's what *Getting Things Done* says too. Actually, *Getting Things Done* says that anything where you have to do more than one thing is a project. Seems picky to me, but you see the point.

The thing with real projects is that they are overwhelming because of their size. Any one project is like its own messy To Do list: you just see these myriad things you know you have to get done. Don't run away from them, don't hide your To Do list, just do this and only this:

> Write down the very next thing you have to do to get this going. Literally, specifically, the very next thing.

For example, my literal and specific next thing after deciding I wanted to write to you was this:

> Look up on Amazon to see if there's already a productivity book for writers

Yes, if there had already been a book, I'd have almost certainly stopped writing, cancelled my plans, moved on. In practice I suspect I'd have bought that book to see whether I thought it worked, whether I thought I could do something usefully different. But that's not the benefit here: the benefit is that this one task would tell me whether or not to continue.

The benefit of that one task is that it is stunningly easy.

Here I am with this entire project ahead of me but all I've got to do is look up Amazon. Once. It's so easy that you know you'd do it. You'd probably do it right there and then. And so, yes, you'd have your answer, but also you've begun this big project. It is underway, you are doing it, and all you've done is the easiest possible thing.

Usually I'm a bit of a fatalist: I believe – and I worked out the maths – that the journey of a thousand miles ends with but 1,999,999 steps. All logic and reason says that looking up Amazon is one piddling step and I'm still left with 1,999,998 so really I've done nothing, I've achieved nothing. But if logic and reason were all that good, we'd be accountants instead of writers. Getting started is big. Getting the first words onto that blank screen is enormous. And if you can trick yourself into it by making the first thing be ridiculously easy, what's not to love?

This is the trick of the next action. It's like it hides the enormity of your project, makes the overall thing seem somehow abstract, and it makes your To Do list a set of very clear, very straightforward and usually very fast things. Call this person, ask this thing, get that fact, write this point.

Next Action always works. Just keep doing the next action – and that means writing your list as a series of next actions. Keep them short, make them clear, spend some time working out what's next. The last time I did a new website, for instance, I had all these plans about what it could do, what it could be for people, but the next actions list began something like this:

> Find a name for the site about productivity for writers
> Buy the domain name from your ISP
> Check hosting price on your current firm and decide whether to stay with them

It wasn't the doddle it seemed because this time finding a name that conveyed what the site was about but was also available to buy was murder. I ended up checking the current price of hosting a new site and deciding to stay with this company before I found the name TheBlankScreen.co.uk. But if my list turned out to be harder to do than I thought, the fact that it looked so straightforward was what got me doing it one bright Sunday morning instead of lying in.

So I started it and I finished it, but I did the list in a different order. I don't mind that, I don't mind that at all: it's no different to having a list of calls and the first person's phone only going to voicemail. For my typical projects, it is enough for me to have these clear tasks and work through them as I can. For you and your projects, that might not be enough.

Serial productivity

Sometimes you have to do your next actions in a very specific order. Look again at the first two tasks in my website:

> Find a name for the site about productivity for writers
> Buy the domain name from your ISP

They mingled because I had to find a name that worked as a domain and was available. So I'd think of a name, check it out, find I couldn't have it, go back to thinking, rinse, repeat. But what I could not do was buy the domain before I had the name. Whatever else happened, the ultimate sequence had to be 1) find name and then 2) buy domain.

That's a sequence of next actions and, if anything, that's the most common type of To Do list project. You can't build a house without planning permission, you can't go abroad without getting a passport. (Long ago, an aunt of mine once flew to Ireland with a gas bill and a bus pass. They were simpler times, though she still needed an aircraft.)

I resist serial projects like this or rather I resist thinking of them this way. I'll write down "Apply for passport" or I'll write down "Look up planning regulations" and I'll know there's a sequence, I'll think about the sequence but at the most I tend to look at the list and decide which one thing is the next action. Which one thing can I do right now.

Recently I've been spending more time looking at sequences. My looking at a list for the next action is no different to churning over a whole To Do list and it would pay me to spend a little effort in organising projects more than I do. The software I use lets me say that this particular project is a serial one and then, if I like, it will only show me what the very next task in the sequence is. But I tend to find that within any one project, some things have to be done in order, others don't.

So my current compromise is to throw a huge list of tasks into a project and then drag them up and down into a kind of rough sequence. Very quick and dirty, very approximate.

I think this one is down to temperament and patience. If you are able to look at a list and sort it into a specific sequence, you go for it. I do think that time spent pointlessly fiddling with your To Do list is a waste but this isn't pointless. Maybe you spend more time on it than I do or maybe you don't, but the time you choose to spend on making a sequence will save you far more time later.

There is a limit, though. At some level, you end up planning what are called dependencies: not just listing a sequence but specifying that this particular task cannot be started until this other one ends. You end up doing things like fixing an end date for the project and working all the tasks backwards to see precisely when you have to start each one. That's like a weaponised To Do list: you'd really need project planning software to do that.

For no great reason, I tend to think project planning is when you have a lot of people to manage and a To Do list is for yourself. I once interviewed some guy who'd won an award for being Project Manager of the Year. It took months to arrange to see him because his To Do list was rubbish. And when I finally got to his door, he was late. And when he appeared, I stood up, stuck out my hand and he walked right by me to the other person he'd double-booked himself for. I thought a rude word.

But I'm at least a little wrong to make this kind of distinction between project planning and To Do lists because it's quite rare that you'll have any task that doesn't involve other people in some way. For instance, I got advice about my website name from colleagues on the Writing West Midlands *Room 204* project. I checked an issue with someone in support at the hosting company.

Very commonly, you'll need someone and just they won't get back to you. This is another thing that comes up in *The Curse of Other People* later in the book but while writing your To Do list, it has this specific impact. You've written this list of things that Can Be Done Now and suddenly that one can't. Not until they reply.

So take it off the list.

I have a separate Waiting list for this and it means I don't have to churn the stuff, I don't have to look at my big list and ever go through the cycle of thinking: can I do this, oh, no, I tried and Bert hasn't phoned back.

The trouble is that it's very easy to create a separate list of things you're waiting for and then leave them waiting, then just never remember to check it. (I've just looked and can breathe out: I only have six things in my Waiting list.)

To avoid them piling up, though, I put them in this waiting list and I add notes such as: "Emailed Bert on the 3rd to ask for my spanner back. Will chase on the 10th." In that situation I can and often do set a start date of the 10th so that I know it's out of my head, out of my way, but will come back on the day that I need it next.

But you don't have to use start dates for that because of the last thing you need to do in To Do lists: reviewing them.

Reviewing rather than panicking

You never review an ordinary To Do list because it's like you're constantly doing that anyway. Every time you pick it up and have to think about whether you've asked Bert already or whether that pharmacy is ever going to open, you're reviewing the list. And the idea of spending time specifically going over it all seems a huge waste.

Perhaps it is. I timed myself yesterday so that I could tell you and I was surprised that it took me nearly two hours to go over my To Do lists. That's a long time out of your working day. But it was a serious review: I looked at every task in every project. And moreover, where the task was just that I was waiting for someone, I emailed them to chase. Where another one was to reply to an email, I replied. I had 53 projects to review and in those two hours I think I did about 20 tasks.

Reviews are very much a *Getting Things Done* idea and the many software applications that are meant to support this GTD approach will insist you do reviews and will also help you. With the one I use for instance, OmniFocus, I can say how often I want to review things. I have a project about pitching for new work, for example, and I want to review that every couple of days because otherwise I get absorbed in the current gig and when it's over suddenly find I have no work. On the other hand, I also have a list of books I want to buy and I'm happy to review that once a year. I know the list is there, I'll choose to look at it when I'm at a bookshop or idling on Amazon, but I'm not forced to review it every day.

So each time you go to do a review, especially in this OmniFocus that I so love, it will show you only the projects that need reviewing. The most I've ever had is that 53 yesterday and that was only because I skipped the previous review session or two. I expect the next one will see me having to review no more than 10 projects and how easy is that next to 53?

Seeing a list of 53 projects and now knowing it'll take two hours to review them makes it very tempting and easy to skip reviewing.

But if writing a To Do list is really about getting tasks out of your head and onto a screen where you can see them, the review is about briefly putting them back inside your noggin so that you can think about them. Your head is rubbish at holding all these tasks but it is fantastic at actually doing them. So reviews are the time to churn: look at a task and think about whether you're ever going to do it or if you can delete it. To think about whether the task is still useful or needs to be clearer. To think about whether you need to add more tasks. (Answer: you do. Always. Never-ending.)

And of course as you're going over your list, you can mark some things as done. I used to be a very automated serial productivity guy who'd find the next action, do it and immediately tick it off the list before going to find the next crisis. Now I often tick things when I've done them but more often I'll come to the review and soon be going yeah, yeah, done that, done this, done the other.

With that two-hour session yesterday, I know I did 20 tasks as I worked through the review and found them, but I also marked off another 15 that I had already done. If you get satisfaction from ticking off one item as done, imagine how great it feels ticking off 35 of the suckers in one go.

It's funny. You used to have this big To Do list with all these things on it and you'd spend the end of each day feeling bad as you'd move these vitally important tasks to tomorrow. Now you've got a much shorter list that only shows you the next action and what Can Be Done. You've actively hidden things away that you can't do or that you started but have to wait for other people. It's like you're ignoring tasks, it's very much like you're choosing to forget them. Because you are. For now. And yet here you are doing the work, you are doing 35 of them and all your projects are moving ahead.

This is what happens when you write a To Do list that is useful. You use it. You get stuff done and that gives you time for your writing.

It also gives you time to be rubbish. And you are. Sometimes. Maybe it's the price of being able to write like a demon some days, but there are always other times when you are writing through treacle. More than any other productivity tip I can ever give you, a clear and specific To Do list of next actions will help the most and will transform your work the most. But it would be good to know in advance when you are going to be a demon and when you are going to be treacle.

There are many things you can do and they're all in the section on *Treacles and Demons*. But sometimes you're the bug, sometimes you're the windshield and whatever you're doing, whenever you're doing it, you get bad days. So that's our next crisis.

Section 2

Bad days

If you're having a bad day today – whether with your writing or at any job holding you back from writing – just do exactly this right now:

- Write down the first five things on your mind.
- Spend the next hour doing the first one. Nothing else.
- In an hour, put that work away mid-thought.
- Spend the next hour doing only the second thing.

Don't look back. You can have tea.

But don't look back.

There's no magic to this, it's just brute-force work and you can do that.

So go do it but then when you have time, when it's no longer such a bad day, come back for the rest of this section.

It's important and it will help you. But not now.

Chapter 5

Coping with bad days

We're not helped as writers by how our work tends to be a feast or a famine. Then we don't help ourselves by spending our working lives strip-mining our emotions and fears to make a piece real. We're also often alone and it's hard to keep perspective when you are. We're also so very often dependent on other work to fund our writing and even if we don't think that other job is important, our employers do.

That's probably not enough to give us a perfect storm for bad days but it. I would be the first to say that there are harder jobs than writing, I'd also be the first to say that there are an awful lot easier ones too.

I've been a freelance writer since 1996 but before then I was working on magazines and computer books on staff during the day and writing drama in the evening. Writing jobs can sap your writing ability more than anything else, but also I think that the skills you have as a writer give you a leg up in any type of job you ever have.

Poets, for instance, are – forgive a stereotype – very experienced in analysing themselves and they are alert to the smallest things. Dramatists – again, broad canvas here – tend to be acutely aware of other people. So both types of writers can see office politics at work. I was once in the cheeriest of production meetings and, by dint of being a writer and by chance of being told enough snippets to build a picture, I was the only one who knew exactly what a cauldron we were in.

It was fascinating, dramatically. There were powerplays going on, there were people who really didn't want to be there, it was exactly as if there were several blatant and semi-blatant agendas underneath the official one. This person wanted that person's job, this other one looking to get out, this third one had a tribunal complaint in about a fourth. No doubt each person there could see something I didn't know, surely they could see something in me that I'm unaware of, but being a writer and specifically being a freelance writer not tied to this particular company meant that I could see all this with a detached eye.

If I'd been working there full time and on staff, I know I wouldn't have been detached, I suspect I would've been embroiled. And it would've been a bigger deal to handle. But I also think I wouldn't have spotted it because I wouldn't have been trying to fit in a day job and an evening's writing, I wouldn't have been managing my time or having to think about how productive I was or wasn't being. I mean, I could even have relaxed and then where would we be?

So I'm going to talk to you about bad writing days both because that's what we're here for and because it will help you in ordinary jobs.

Except. There is one thing:

> If you have a non-writing job in the day, start writing on your commute home or at the very latest as soon as you get back.
>
> Definitely do not eat. Once you've eaten that evening meal, you're through.

There is one rather big exception. If you're the one doing the cooking for the family, you're not going to ask them to wait. Conceivably you could feed 'em, get to writing and then cook for yourself later but that's just a waste of your time on so many levels. So do what you need to do and when everyone's eaten or you've got the kids to bed, start writing. It will be hard to start, there's no getting around that. But, hey, at least you're fed and maybe it's now wine o'clock too.

Whether it's hard at the end of the evening after seeing to your family or it's hard earlier on because you've just had a long day at work, go to the keyboard and say you'll just do a few minutes. You won't. You'll do more than that. And once you've got started, it will be worth it.

Bad Writing Days

Maybe you have too much to do. Maybe it's the opposite and you have nothing. Every project you had out there has just been rejected and you feel like you're having to start all over again. You are. So one quick way to slightly alleviate a certain type of bad day is to always have something else out with an editor or a producer. You can't do it every time and the chance of how book schedules work or magazine lead times, Cannes and offers rounds means you will sometimes get that massive pile landing at the same moment. But reduce the odds by at least starting the next thing before you finish the current one. If you get breaks, take them midway through some projects rather than always in between them. It's not the greatest bandaid in the world that you're deep into the next thing when a rejection comes, but it is the only bandaid in the world.

Whether you're starting over from nothing or you have too much to do, you can be overwhelmed with the certainty that actually there's no point beginning it at all. You think that you cannot get everything finished and you're certain that you can't do another giant writing project today.

As a species, we writers are also a bit prone to depression. People who don't have this seem to believe that it can be fixed by a tickling stick when of course you can really be paralysed by depression at any time. There isn't a connection between how happy you are yet dammit if there isn't a strong connection the other way: you cannot make depression better but you can readily, easily make it worse with bad news. Depression on a bad day is an anvil with a knife on it.

So maybe you're facing this busy mountain or this empty valley, maybe you're low and if you are depressed then you'll be feeling it physically too, so everything screams at you that it is impossible to get through this. That it is impossible to get this work done or get this work started.

The knife is that it's true.

You may not be in the mood to hear this and you may be under such pressure that you don't have time to hear it, but you will not magically get everything done.

Sorry. I'd like to give you two aspirin and tell you to call me in the morning but you're a writer, I can't fool you. And the sooner that we can accept that overwhelming impossibility is impossible for a reason, the sooner we can start whelming.

So here's the thing. You won't get it all done but you will get it all started and the time you're spending now in a tizzy or having to hold your chest to stop the anxiety will be much better spent starting the work. Just starting it. Just the first word. At the beginning, that looks pointless enough to make you sick. But getting started in any way is like ignition: it takes more power to start an engine than to keep it going. And once the engine is going, it wants to keep moving forward.

And what's more, you may have these pressures and burdens because you're a writer but you have certain advantages too. You're a writer: you can fool yourself. I just need you to fool yourself in a certain way.

You know how parents who also have demanding jobs – so they've really got two demanding jobs – can actually find the office work relaxing? There are all these issues of balancing work and life, family and career, and if you have kids you want to be with them. But in the moment, day to day, when you get to the office, it actually feels relaxing. Because you're supposed to be there. This is exactly what you are supposed to be doing and there is no option about it for the next eight to ten hours. A huge amount of misery comes from constant struggles over whether you're doing the right thing at the right time: you burn up the day being anxious instead of doing anything. So those office hours may dump incredible stresses on you but they take this one away and it's gigantic.

It's not as if it's true that you have no choice about being there, either. If your kid had an accident you'd be out of that office meeting at lightspeed and bollocks to anyone who complains about it. But there is enough truth in it, enough reality to the timetable and the contract that it works. What you need to do is conjure up that same truth for yourself today. Especially if today is a bad day.

That Kwik-E-Mart solution at the start of this chapter is really just doing that with brute force: it is simply conjuring a timetable. The trick of it is that if you accept that for the next hour you are only and exclusively doing this one particular thing, it stops you thinking about all the other stuff. That other stuff is not your job, not your concern. This is. It is a trick and it isn't automatic or easy, and it also has the kicker that somewhere around 40 minutes in you will long to get out of this bloody thing and go on to the next or anything else. But if you make yourself work on for those last 20 minutes, it's hard enough that it helps make this feel real. It also makes you deep-mine yourself and you can end up writing the best material in the last stretch.

Which you'd think would mean you should then carry on until you finish.

No.

At the end of the hour, stop it and move on. Don't look back at that last hour, don't pat yourself on the back or criticise yourself, it's done. Gone. And now don't plan the next hour, don't look ahead to the rest of the day, just take that next thing from the top of your list and that is solely and exclusively what you are doing now.

The odds are that you will finish some things in each of these hours and if you do, great. Go on to the next. Just be certain you've finished, don't tell yourself you've kinda, sorta done or that this will do. Finish and move on or don't.

It's almost better when you don't finish in the hour. Because it's like novelists who end the day by writing the first line of the next chapter and so know that will get them started tomorrow morning. You probably don't have time to walk away from all of your writing for a day, but doing this brutal cease-and-desist at the end of the hour means you're leaving that project with energy and with it all alive in your head. You want to continue it – and isn't that better than an hour ago when you didn't even want to start? – and it means you're ending the hour before you fade away. All that energy goes into the next project and then at the end of the hour on that, you're out again before you burn out.

I'm not saying you have to be Sellotaped to your keyboard for the hour, all writing is fuelled by vices and on a bad day you need that caffeine or sugar more than ever. But bring the biscuits and the coffee to the desk and get on with it. Sod crumbs. Clean up the mess later, you're working now.

At the end of the five hours, you will not have completed your work, you will not have met all your pressures and deadlines, you won't have magically launched an entire new writing project.

But you will be so far ahead of where you were at the start. And typically you'll still have time left in the day to finish some of the five. It is an awful lot easier to finish some things when everything has so much already done in it.

You would imagine that the aim of all this is to get these things done but really it's about the immense psychological benefits of being that far forward. You had these five things that were impossible, paralysing mountains and now you have these same five things but you're energetic and alive to them all – and you have made substantial progress too.

Substantial is a relative thing. Stephen King does 2,000 words every morning. James Joyce used to say that "three sentences" was a great day. If you do all this productive concentrating and the product of each hour's productivity is a single page per project then yes, so, and? That's a single page you didn't have at the start.

It also doesn't have to be five things, by the way. And it doesn't even have to be an hour at a time. That's what works for me because I seem to function best in hour chunks – and my problem is going on to the next hour without a break – but your mileage may vary. This is similar to the Pomodoro technique which says work for twenty-five minutes, stop for five, work for twenty-five. I like that but it doesn't seem to fit me as well as the hours do: I find those hours long enough to be hard and so feel like work yet then also long enough to make some clear progress on most of the types of writing I do.

If you like the idea of using the internet to help you fight distractions, use Google for your hours or for your Pomodoro 25-minute technique. Where you would normally type in something you want to search for, type "Set a timer for 25 minutes" instead. And watch it work.

Shape of the Day

There is something handy for me about doing it in hours rather than 25 minute slices, though. When things are at their very worst, I will take a minute or three the night before to write what I call the *Shape of the Day*. It's a timetable, really, and in this very moment telling you that I suddenly realise that it's exactly like my old school schedule. I'm a bit shocked at that: I was a poor student in a bad school, I thought the only thing I got from it was the journalist's ability to play politics. But apparently I also got a work ethic.

This is how my *Shape of the Day* timetable works. I write from 5am weekdays and on very bad days I will sketch out a shape that starts then and runs mostly in hours until maybe noon or 3pm. I know I'll be working on after that but I run out of steam with the plan. I'll also run out of steam with the work but on certain types of very, very bad days you don't get the option to stop.

All I do is list out the times and a topic or title: no details, no notes. This is a typical shape of the day when I'm mostly writing books:

05:00-06:00 Current book
06:00-07:00 Current script
07:00-07:30 Mortar*
07:30-08:00 Current book
08:00-09:00 Make breakfasts, lunches, dishwasher loading/unloading
09:00-10:00 Current book
10:00-11:00 Mortar
11:00-12:00 Calls and pitches
12:00-13:00 Current book
13:00-14:00 Lunch (incl reading for current book)
14:00-15:00 Current script and re-reading the day's work

*Mortar is my shorthand term for all the stuff that keeps everything together. I'll definitely do emails, certainly check through my OmniFocus To Do task list and make sure there's nothing on the calendar that I've forgotten. Later Mortars will include phone calls.

I really do write it all out as, say, 05:00-06:00, full-on 24-hour-clock military time and of course anyone sane would just write 5am start this, 6am start that. Or anyone really sane would obviously be writing something like 10am start. I'm not proud of my 5am starts, but I'm afraid I am a bit smug. Unbearable, actually. Good thing you're not up then to see it.

For me, doing the times out in full this way makes it easy to see at a glance where I am, especially if circumstance mean I have to add in a quarter or a half hour on something new that comes up. As I did there in that typical example: whatever day I did that for real, I changed the 07:00-08:00 entry into two half-hour ones and broke up the work. I don't go further than that, I don't plan, say, in five-minute chunks because I don't have the time, I don't have the patience or the discipline – and because that would make a huge list each day that would be tricky to simply glance at and move on. The point of it all is to do exactly that: make checking that shape of the day list a glance rather than a chore.

Plus, I now have a TextExpander snippet: whatever I'm doing on my

Mac, if I type ";shape" with the semi-colon but without the quotes it instantly writes out all of this for me:

05:00-06:00
06:00-07:00
07:00-08:00
08:00-09:00
09:00-10:00
10:00-11:00
11:00-12:00
12:00-13:00
13:00-14:00 Lunch
14:00-15:00
15:00-16:00
16:00-17:00
17:00-18:00

Notice the Lunch bit in the middle. I put that in so that it would always be in the list: I used to forget to eat and when you're under the cosh then lunch is the easiest thing to cross off your list but it's important. And like everything else in this whole book, spending a little time now on something saves you a lot of time later. So taking ten minutes to make a sandwich and then reading while you eat means the work you do later will be better. You get the nourishment, of course, but you've also had a complete break, a separation from the tasks that are so overwhelming you.

TextExpander is Mac-only software, by the way, but whatever computer you write on, there are utilities like this which can help immensely and could add up to a lot of money.

I am very much a software fan: it is specifically software that has meant I can do the work I do and that you and I can talk like this. Software is so useful and so great that there is no question that there are applications and utilities that will transform your working life. But that doesn't mean you need any of it or that all of it will work for everyone.

Here's a bad example. An unfair example. There is a popular iPhone and iPad app called *Daily Routine* by Jaysen Marais. It's not only popular, it's won awards – and it's shockingly like my *Shape of the Day*. You set up that shape or that routine and throughout the day you can see what you're supposed to be doing. It's colour-coordinated, there's a continuous running timer so you can instantly see you've got another 59 minutes on this hour. And setting the routine up is actually, genuinely fun. Run your finger up and down the schedule and it expands and contracts slots to make them more readable. It's functional but it moves like liquid and you cannot, cannot resist just wiggling the thing up and down.

I wiggled. On the day I bought it, Daily Routine went straight onto my very front screen of my iPhone. But today it's nowhere to be seen. Sorry, Jaysen. I think this app works best if you have pretty set routines. Definitely if you know that Tuesday is always when you go to a London office and so you have these set travel times, those set meetings, that kind of thing. My days are less predictable and I was more creating countless routines to follow than I was trying to make sure I stuck to an existing one.

I ended up with endless routines and even then I was always altering them. So there's this highly-praised, extremely well made app that does exactly what I need but it isn't quite right for me. I'm all for spending time now to save it later but if something isn't working, I'd rather move on. Equally, when it is working for me, I stay. So for instance you'd need to wrap Primacord explosive around my waist before you'd get me away from OmniFocus.

Software is different for different people, routines are different, the ways we concentrate and the things we have to write are all different. So while I want you to keep schedules and plans to a true minimum, I know they will help you.

Going too far

If I'm not proud of getting up to write at 5am, I am actively embarrassed by this next thing: I sometimes keep a log of what I'm doing. So far, so what? It was even reasonable, verging on sensible, when I was trying to work out my treacle and demon times: I could look at this log and see I did a huge amount on Wednesday morning and absolutely nothing worth a damn on Thursday afternoon.

But something strange happened. I started writing down what I did in the most extreme detail. Well, the notes per se were short but I'd put the times in and I could be doing minute to minute. I've just looked back at the latest one of these I did and it has an entry about every twenty minutes on average, but there are sections where it is minute to minute.

Actually, I've just looked back over the last dozen or so and it's not as OCD as I thought. Very often it's got about ten entries and then the last one is something like "09:18 left for meeting" and then I don't note anything else for the rest of the day.

The most common entry in this log is something like "Hour begins 05:17". That's when I work an hour without stopping: I get iTunes to play me an hour's worth of music (over headphones, I'm not inconsiderate) or maybe I tell Siri on my iPhone to set a timer for an hour. Either way, I write until the music stops or the alarm sounds. Sometimes I've noticed after an hour that I've been wearing headphones yet forgot to start any music. And very often I just write on past the hour. I really mean it about the importance of stopping after sixty minutes but when the deadline doesn't allow that or somehow when your hours are that early in the day, I'm good with carrying on.

So the joint equal most common entry in my log is something like "Hour ends 08:01". It's the same "hour":

> Hour begins 05:17
> Hour ends 08:01

I don't know why that tickles me but I do know that I wanted to tell you that first so that you don't think I am an absurd anally retentive type who is writing down every action of every minute as I work. That you think I am – gasp – trying to multitask.

If I'm this uncomfortable telling you all that, you'd think I could just select this section and delete it. You'd never know it was here and you could continue believing me to be just roguishly handsome. But on the very, very worst days, this log has had an unexpectedly powerful benefit and that's why I want you to know about it.

This daily log makes me edgy when I'm not working.

It makes me really edgy when I haven't done anything for a few minutes. If I even take a tea break, I find the fact that the log is there listing, proving that I haven't done anything in two, three, six, eight minutes, I run back to the desk. I have had occasions when I have rung an editor to pitch an article specifically so that I could write it down in the log.

Maybe it's like having someone to account to for your time. But it is a constant nudge and at the end of the day, you can often look back and actually feel like you've achieved something with your time. When you're writing a book, it's often hard to see what you've done: the easy and obvious measure of progress is the word count but for huge periods of time you're not writing anything at all. Then equally often you're rewriting so at the start of the day the passage might be 5,000 words and at the end of the day you have totally changed every syllable – but it's still 5,000 words.

So if I can see in my log that I transcribed this interview, found that document, read that source, phoned that contact, planned that bit, rewrote that section, I feel like I've worked. I don't feel as if I've been playing at being a writer.

I think that this Daily Log I do is the thing I recommend least. Have a try if you're not already shaking your head. And if you do want to do it, let me tell you that I write mine in Evernote plus I have some TextExpander snippets that make it a bit quicker. (If I type "ttime", with a double t and without the quotes, for instance, it will enter the current time. So I'm not forever looking up the time, I'm finishing a call or a page, skipping over to Evernote, typing "ttime" and a couple of words in order to enter something like "11:07 Got magazine commission".)

So, just to be clear, I sometimes plot out the *Shape of the Day* and then I might also write a Daily Log. The log helps enough that I do it quite often, if sometimes in the very least detail – "05:00 up, 18:00 collapse" – and the shape plotting is only for bad days. But if you're now thinking I like rules, I can see why, but actually, not so much.

No rules, please, we're writers

I'm a writer who doesn't like outlines and hates writing treatments because I feel I'd rather explore the story on the page. But when I do a *Doctor Who* audio for Big Finish, for example, I have to do a treatment because that's what determines whether I get to go on to write the script. Similarly, I'm not a big fan of Robert McKee's rules but without my trying, the drama I write does tend to fall into the three acts he says it should.

Then within a story we set up certain rules for ourselves and our characters. For example, you know that audiences would feel more than a little cheated if the blind watchmaker with his seven sons – sure an' they all have a tale to tell – gets out of trouble because he can suddenly see.

We don't like rules, we don't like constraints, but we use them. We make them. Productivity is just making some rules for ourselves. And sticking to them, even on very bad days.

Listen, I don't know if it'll help you to know, but this chapter was written on one such very bad day and I did it in precisely the way I just told you. By the end of the hour on it, I wasn't finished of course but I was 2,000 words in and it felt like at least I hadn't wasted the time. It also strip-mined how I was feeling about anxiety over deadlines so maybe it was in fact the best day to write it. And I did leave that hour with energy, I did go on to the next hour making phone calls and dealing with contracts and bills and people. I really didn't want to do any of that but I did it. As ever, the thing with doing stuff is that then it's done. And you can get on to the next crisis.

Full disclosure: I also left the first hour dying with hunger. And rather than a total stop and change to the next item, I wrote two lines about what I should be covering whenever I came back to this chapter.

In fact, for the fullest of full disclosure, what I wrote was:

> Add something about your TextExpander snippet but keep it short because you're doing a chapter on software later; remember that stuff from your blog about how you tried to use software and this one time it just didn't work for you. Too much effort.

So that's not sticking to my rule of stopping mid-thought, mid-sentence.

But this was the first of the five hours and by the end of it, I was already feeling the benefit. Already feeling less overwhelmed and so more able to deal with the rest. You can't avoid bad days but you can insure against them at least a little by giving yourself more time. And you can take steps to head some problems off at the pass by trying to make sure that a bad day doesn't fall on the very worst of days.

There are no guarantees for this one but next we're going to look at your week. And at least if the anvil and the knife strike on a day when you're a demon, it's a bit better than when you're covered in treacle.

Seriously, if you quote that last paragraph in a review I will look like a nutter.

Section 3

Demons and Treacles

The definition of a writer is someone who doesn't write. If somebody is forever scribbling and it's all effortless joy and happiness then they're not writers and I am safe to say that to you because there's not one single chilly chance they'll ever read this book.

The rest of us have a much more volatile time with writing: we want to do it, writing is an illness for us, but it's hard and sometimes you want to run away. Unfortunately, the harsh truth is that sometimes you should. Sometimes you are simply not going to write well at all and the time you spend now, the effort you put in to writing anyway, is not just worthless, it's damaging. You write rubbish, it costs you sweat, ultimately you can't help but think writing is a mug's game and anyway sod this for a game of soldiers.

The even harsher truth is often you have no choice. The section on *Bad Days* covered what to do then but now it's how to minimise the chances and the impact of that damage. How to know in advance that this, right now, is a bad time to write – and what you can do with this time to help later.

Chapter 6

Finding when you can and can't write

We've talked a lot about tasks but just for now, I want you to forget that and think about time instead. Specifically this: think about what you did last week. Write me a really quick list of one-liners about each of the seven days last week and what happened. Seriously quick: "Monday - meetings all day", "Saturday – DIY". Tuesday afternoon – "tryst".

It's an odd thing but we tend to think more and remember more about events than tasks we've done or items we've craved. I'm not sure whether it's a good or a bad thing, but we'll remember that time we got locked up in prison on the Lower East Side far longer than we'll remember taking out that extra credit card to pay the bail before we fled the country under assumed names. Or maybe that's just me.

But when I ask you to do that list about last week, you probably did say that Wednesday was when you were at that office or Thursday was when you worked from home. I'll bet you money that you didn't write "Tuesday – thought about it and decided to call my heroine Myriad Moore", "Saturday – revised scene 12 to take out the slander".

Use this strange thing about our minds and memories. Use it to look ahead to next week and write me a slightly longer list about that. Whatever is happening, whatever will actually happen, you already know what you think next week is going to be like. You know what your big commitments are. You know that you've got a dentist appointment on Thursday, you know that you can lie on the beach until Friday when you've got to fly home. You know that you have a pitch meeting or an annual review and you know when they are. Or at least you know a lot of them.

At risk of making this an expensive chapter, I'm going to bet money again that you'll find writing this prediction of the week very easy – and that every single thing you write down was determined by someone else. The dental surgery's next available appointment. That producer who offered you a pitch meeting.

I'm betting even more that you didn't think about how you'll feel at each of these points. Maybe you sunk at the thought of the annual review. But if that's on Friday at 9am then that's where you'll be, that's what you'll be doing and that's when you'll be doing it.

I can't change that. And neither you nor I can change the fact Friday 9am may be the worst possible time for us. You could make it worse – say by having a leaving party on Thursday night and going straight from the pub to your desk in the morning – or you could make it better by exercise and other fads. But in general, we go up and down throughout the week and we carry on working regardless. Because we have to.

What we can change is the work we do and when we do it.

This is true whether you're talking about writing, whether you work at home full time as a writer or whether you work full time at something else and have to write in the evenings. Especially when you have a 9-5 job, your job is to be there 9-5 and you have to work because that's what you're hired to do. But few jobs outside factory work or certain retail ones require you to be doing completely precisely the same thing every minute of that working week. And then if you do have a job like that, the rest of your life is chaos in comparison and you can do some juggling there.

It's a fact that website traffic goes up on a Friday afternoon because office workers are slowing down and thinking about the weekend ahead. It must be nice to be able to slow down just because it's Friday but for a significant number of people, that's what happens. So you would be crazy to expect a three-hour, in-depth, page-by-page story conference to start at 4pm on a Friday. You'd probably also be mad to schedule any meeting for 8am Monday.

So there's the start and the end of the typical working week already affected, already bad spots to do real work. But those examples are still external ones, they're still coming from other people. What's most important is the schedule within you: a schedule you don't tend to think about and maybe you don't even want to, but is there.

You're an early riser or you're a late-night jazz club sort. It takes you a long time to write anything or you dash stuff very quickly. You're really annoying and grumpy in the mornings and you're absolutely the life of the party at lunchtimes.

More likely, you shuffle between all of these and you can't guess how you're going to be at any one point in the day

Try anyway. Try predicting it. First, go back to your list from last week and for each day write down next to each point whether you were a demon writer or a treacle one. I'm not trying to create a term here – Demons and Treacles sounds like a Dan Brown novel – but for speed and gross over-simplification just write demon or treacle by each line. If your list has morning/afternoon/evening parts to it, great: treacle or demon against each one.

Now forget what you did and just copy over that list of treacles and demons to what you're doing next week. Only the demon/treacle line. If you were a demon last Monday, write down that you'll be a demon next Monday too. Treacle Wednesday last week equals treacle Wednesday this week. It isn't true that you're exactly the same each week but it's true enough and this is useful enough to be a starting point.

Particularly because now you need to look at what you're going to be doing on each of those days next week. If you wrote that Thursday is the day you get so depressive that you could cheerfully destroy Tokyo then look at what you're expecting to do that day. If the only thing on the calendar is the dentist appointment then fine. Nobody says you have to enjoy a dentist appointment, you just have to go. But if you've written treacle next to when you have your annual review, is there really no way you can reschedule it? Maybe not, but it's worth a try.

And equally, if your Monday afternoon is your greatest demon-writing time of the entire week but you've now got a HR seminar scheduled for then, get out of it if you possibly can.

Most important of all: find those great demon-writing points. If one is Saturday morning and you have nothing else you have to do, that's when you're going to write. And you can bet that this is exactly when other things will come up, partly because you're on fire and you are able to get a lot done then. Some of these pop-up distractions are your fault: it's you saying yes, I could solve that plot problem but, gosh, the guttering really must be fixed right now. Other incursions into your time will be other people, especially if it just looks like you're playing at your computer.

Whatever time your best writing is, protect it. That sounds so obvious but you don't do it now: you let other things take over and oftentimes you absolutely have to. But it's what I said at the very start of this book: nothing in this will improve your writing but all of it will get you more time to write. This is that more time. Get this. Protect this.

First, find your times. Then move heaven and Earth to get all non-writing work out of that time. You do that partly by how I'm going to tell you to deal with the treacle days, partly by locking yourself away from other people and from the internet.

But there is an important problem.

An important problem

Let's say you are an extreme case. You work five days at a non-writing job, you're a parent and you have one hour in your week in which to write. You regularly have to sacrifice that hour too. But now you've done all this productivity stuff, all the detritus of the week is done and out of the way, you have a cool sixty minutes ahead of you in which all you have to do is write.

This is where it is the most unfair that writing is hard. Everything is set, everything is done, it's just down to you now and the pressure you feel is paralysing. It's especially hard because your whole family knows this is your writing time and actually they don't understand it, they just tolerate it. Non-writers don't get it. I'm sure there are things that we don't get but I don't know what they are because I don't get them. But this is why it's good for you and I to get to talk about this, it's why supportive writing groups can be such a help.

It's also when productivity tricks help. I don't really see any of this stuff as a trick, but oftentimes I'll do something small that I know is small, that

I tell myself is a trivial little trick, yet I also know that it'll probably make me go on to do more. So I'm fooling myself into being more productive and while part of me wishes I weren't so easily and readily gullible, it works.

I'll show you my ways if you'll show me yours. Mine are in the chapter on *The Curse of You* and anything you can tell me back on william@theblankscreen.co.uk will be eagerly eaten up.

But for now, for the treacles and demons, understand that you're not programmable and you can't be scheduled: even when you expect to be writing well and you have the time, you can treacle up. Sometimes you can just play through the pain and keep writing, sometimes you're better off going away. But every single time, this is not a failure, it is not proof that you can't write, it is proof that you are a complex little soldier. And it's proof that if you can clear more time for your writing, you can have the capacity to walk away when necessary.

Walk away

If you've just got yourself this hour or this day and it's not working, look around you. When you've got people who have agreed to leave you alone while you write, don't go talk to them now. Try not to even leave your desk.

So when I say walk away and you're thinking it's a lovely day, garden, sunshine, film festival, chocolate ice cream and sleep, I'm usually thinking walk your mind away from the specific writing project. And use that time to do other things.

You will still have some ordinary, boring, urgent, vital, brainless-but-demanding tasks that have nothing to do with writing but can be done at your keyboard. So do them. Write that email, fill out that form, anything you can.

Because the great thing about tasks is that when they're done, they're gone. Anything you can ever clear out of the way now stops being something else facing you in the future. So if you can't create, get shovelling the rubbish out of the way so that you clear time and when you can create, you're not up to your neck in other tasks.

The wide-open week

Officially, this is the opposite of having to fit your one hour of writing a week in around all your other work. This is when you are writing all week and next week and the week after. Unofficially, it's exactly the same.

Whenever you're trying to get writing work, you want to be commissioned. When you are commissioned, suddenly that other pet project of yours starts calling you. Especially when you think about your deadlines, especially when you have been buried in writing the commission for a long time. Much as I advocate doing one thing at a time and much as this is probably the case when you really should do that, sometimes it is necessary to just write something else for a bit.

But just nipping off to do another script when you feel like it will always make you feel guilty and you will nearly always be right to feel that. You know that you're already careful on Facebook when you're commissioned, that you don't go saying what a great day out in the sunshine you've had when your editor is on your friends list and thinks you're working. Only, that editor might not see your update. You might get away with it. If only you weren't policing yourself and feeling guilty.

The worst thing about guilt, though, is that it takes time. Maybe a lot, maybe a little, it all depends on you, but there is at least the niggle when you recognise that you probably ought to be feeling guilty. So get rid of the guilt and you get rid of at least the niggle, at most the regular, recurring, never-ending worrying about it.

The easy bit

First, do nothing. We can all do nothing and do it very well. We could do Nothing for England, especially given enough biscuits and tea. But I mean forget all this productivity, forget all your deadlines, forget everything except the work and get writing. For a day. It would be nice if you could do this for a week and if you ever can, you go for it, but we need a day at least.

It doesn't matter whether the day is actually spent writing, as in pressing those gorgeous keys on the keyboard, or research, dictation, interviewing, anything. As long as it's part of your writing job then do it and at the end of the day, look at what you've done. You might find that my Daily Log idea helps with that, you might find that my Daily Log idea is the raving of a deluded eejit. But whatever way you can, measure what you did today.

This is not about quality. It's not about increasing your page count by so many percent every day until we reach next May and you're writing War and Peace sequels every hour. This is about honesty. We can all be faster and we can all be better: even though I'm talking to you about productivity, bollocks to being faster. Put all your effort into writing better – and use all these productivity tools to give yourself more time in which to do it. Tools. That's a better word than tricks. I'm having that.

If you did write all day and you can see a pile of paper or more likely see the word count, great. Put the biscuits back down. You've got a word count. Or if you did research, if you made calls, you have some note of what you did.

Here's the thing. If you do exactly that tomorrow and tomorrow and tomorrow, how long before your current writing project is done? Forget deadlines. Forget that you will have these treacle and demon days, just pretend that it's a maths problem.

I tend to get quite mechanical about stories: I don't think you can calculate your way out of a plot point but I will go around the options like it's a survey. What's the worst thing that can happen to this character? And this one? What if this happened to that other character instead? Honestly, it never once gives me an answer. But making it an abstract, even easy technical problem instead of a nebulous, difficult drama one, somehow also makes it so that I can trundle it all around in my head. It doesn't give me an answer, yet I end up with an answer.

So in the same way, mechanically extrapolating out how long your writing work will take you is a help. It's less of a help if you have no idea what the final writing work will look like or what its page- or word-count will be. It can't give you the answer, but you will end up with an answer.

Now use that. If it's going to take you a year to finish the novel, now you know. And you also know where you are each day. You know when you're ahead and so when you can relax a bit.

Never forget that this is all a trick, an approximation. But it works. And I'll take anything if it works.

It is a long term thing, though. It's not so great in the short term, such as this week. You can use the fact that you should be so many words or so many pages along by Friday but in practice your bigger issue is in getting the most out of your time. It's divide and conquer: arrange your week so that you are doing the right thing at the right time.

Treacles and demons are a help. Finding your best writing time is superb. But we all start with a fallacy: we assume our working week is the same as everybody else's and is the same as we've always had it. Hard as it is to make ourselves grasp sometimes, we do not work a 9-5 existence. We might also work 9-5 on something, it might even be writing, but writing is not a timetabled job, it is an illness and we don't stop.

The quite brutal bit

All of this treacle and demon stuff works because on the one hand, you know roughly how you're going to feel this week because you felt that way last week, and on the other, you can still make use of time even when it's treacle-based. But that supposes that your schedule never changes. Actually, it doesn't. Not as much as you imagine.

Obviously if you have a 9 to 5 job, Monday to Friday, that's a whole chunk of unchanging schedule but even if you don't, we tend to fall into patterns. Next time you go into a supermarket, notice who goes in at the same time as you. The same people will be leaving that supermarket when you are. Part of this is that supermarkets are amazing machines for getting you through and out quickly – and spending the absolute maximum possible in that time – but you don't notice it and we don't notice our repeating schedules.

Therefore, if you go back over last week in excruciating hour-by-hour detail, you will find a gigantic amount is exactly the same next week.

So change the rules. Change the hours. Look at when you get up, when you go to bed and change them. You already do this when you're on a deadline but because you're on a deadline, you don't have time to notice much other than the adrenalin, the coffee and the panic. Move your bedtime back an hour for a week and write then. Get up an hour earlier for a week and write then.

Some years ago, Angela was ill and I segued into a new schedule. I'd get up a few hours before she did in order to work, then I'd look after her during the day and evening, then I'd work a few hours after she went to bed. I feel bad saying it was hard because, after all, I wasn't ill, I wasn't the one going through all this, but I admit it was hard. Sometimes I'd long for her to go to bed as the night wore on and I had more I needed to do.

She's much better now, thank you for asking, and my schedule went back to normal. But I'd found that those early mornings were remarkably productive. So last year when I was on a *Doctor Who* deadline, I tried it again: I got up at 5am for each of the days I was writing that script. Then I immediately went back to my preferred late-night William ways. I don't drink, I don't smoke, but I feel like a jazz rebel because I blossom at night.

Except.

Truly, I love being a late night person. I even like the writing at 2am or whenever it is. And Twitter was the most gorgeous invention for late-night writing: you can take a two-minute break and be nattering away to fellow writers for several hours beyond the time you intended.

However, the cold fact was that my writing wasn't all that good late at night. Or at least I was finding that I had to revise it a great deal more than material I did during the mornings.

So while it crippled me to do this and I don't specifically recommend it to you, I now get up to write at 5am weekdays.

Bear with me on this

What I do really recommend is that you experiment to find the times you write best. This is all happy bollocks when you're writing for a living and have no choice but to work all day. But whatever your situation, there are times that suit you better than others and if you can find them, you can use them.

So yes, do this later bedtime or earlier rise. See if you can work at lunchtimes: I've had some success doing that even during full writing days as I step away to another project and know that I have only one hour and two ham sandwiches in which to work on this thing. Similarly, see if there's anything you can change about your typical commute. When I got my first book contract I was also committed to a magazine and website job in London and I would drive there and back at least once a week. I'm struggling to remember the details now but it was something like a two-hour drive to London and a four-hour drive back. I do remember that I tended to go out after work there because traffic meant there was no difference between my setting off for home at 7pm or at 9pm. I'd still be back around 11pm or midnight.

But that's a lot of time, it's six to eight hours in a day and those were wrapped around the eight or nine hours working for the magazine. So there was extremely little chance I could work on the book on one of my London days. And I had to. Consequently, I wrote every lunchtime and for a while I ditched the car in favour of trains and coaches. I remember falling asleep on a train coming home and waking up to see thirty men pressed against the window making faces at me. Either we'd stopped at Birmingham International train station and the AC/DC concert had just ended at the Arena or they were really fit men who were running fast.

I did sometimes sleep deliberately. And if I'm honest, sometimes I'd size up the rest of the carriage or the coach and decide not to get out all my expensive computer gear.

But at the end of three months or so, I'd written the book and discovered that I had saved many hundreds of pounds in petrol. It was a surprise but it was the kind of surprise that turns you pale because you think of how long you've been driving to London, how long you've been spending hundreds of pounds. I don't want to say the word decade to you, but I just have. I never drove to London again. I stopped driving to the magazine and I sold my car.

So I'd started out trying to carve some more time for my writing and I ended up saving a huge amount of cash, the planet probably liked me more, and most of all, I ended up with a book.

I think one key thing there is that I got myself all this extra time by changing my schedule and avoiding driving, but the second key thing is that it took me some months. At the start, I couldn't see how to make a difference and at the end I can't see how I ever used to waste that much time and cash. The middle was easy because I was too busy with the book to really pay any attention to how I was changing my time. So when I did notice it and I did see how useful it had been, I'd got used to doing it.

You have to try something new and then you have to give it time to work.

I learnt that over the London book business and I learnt it again over beating a *Doctor Who* deadline and I learnt it a third time while looking after Angela but still I had to fight myself to do what I knew needed to be done. As I say, I now get up at 5am to write and it works very well for me. But to do it, I needed trickery. Brutal trickery. Maybe this says more about me than it should, but I needed it and it's worked. So far.

The Brutal £1 Bucket Method

Here's the thing. I only get up at 5am on weekdays and if I know in advance that I'm going to be travelling, I'll book that day off, so to speak. I've had speaking engagements that I knew would mean I didn't get home and I wouldn't calm down until after midnight. So I would book those next mornings off. A couple of times I've had such heavy colds that I've known the day before that I wouldn't be working at all, let alone at 5am, so again I mentally book those off. I took a holiday once too.

You have to try these crazy things.

But on a typical, ordinary, majority Monday to Friday, my alarm goes off at 5am. And if I get up, I put a £1 coin in a plastic bucket by the bed.

Fine. You get the idea: seeing that grow into a pile of coins is great. But that's not the trick.

The trick is what happens if I don't get up at 5am, if I sleep in or if I give up and turn over, pulling the blanket over my head. You're thinking that I don't put a £1 coin in and yes, you're absolutely right, but that's not it either. That's not all.

Now you're thinking, okay, maybe he takes a £1 coin out and you're getting there but you're still not right, you're still being too nice.

What really happens is that if I fail to get up at 5am on weekdays, I empty the whole bucket and start again. From zero.

I'm not quite sure what I'd do with the coins I'd be throwing away but I would be throwing them away: I'd give them to someone or something, anything that didn't benefit me. Anything that in some way punished me. But you can tell from the way I'm saying this that I don't know what I'd do because I haven't emptied that bucket yet. As of this moment, I have 131 pound coins in there and there are now mornings when I get up at 5am and nearly forget the coin.

I count that as having got used to an idea. I think I also count it as madness but it works for me and having got up, I get more done and it is better. Dammit.

The easier Seinfeld method

I think I'd heard of the Seinfeld method before, but I was told about it again by someone who knew I was doing this Brutal £1 Bucket Method. Why they didn't tell me until I was seventy coins in to that, I don't know. But the principle is the same. You just might like this one a lot better.

In comedian and writer Seinfeld's method, you take a giant wall-planner-sized calendar and you cross off each day that you write. The aim is to write every day and after a little while, you have a row or a chain of crosses and suddenly any day you don't write, there's this awful white blank space in the middle of the chain. Seinfeld's advice: "Don't break the chain". That's it.

Actually, if his is less harsh than mine, it does have a benefit that mine doesn't: every time you look at that calendar you can see progress but you can also see each failure. In theory I can see absolute failure because I'd have an empty bucket, but it's harder to see success because the difference between 100 £1 coins and 101 of them is not all that visible.

His technique is also specifically about making you write where mine is geared to specifically making me get up. I wash quickly, I get a mug of tea, a pint of water and a banana and I do write. But sometimes you see that pile of waiting emails and you think you'll just answer one of those. And then the next thing you know, it's 8am and time for breakfast.

So my Brutal method has its weaknesses but it also plainly has its strengths as I've kept on doing it and I now can't imagine stopping. I can dream about stopping, but I can't imagine it.

If you really pushed me, I would say that 5am writing would be good for you. I'm almost certain. You get a good five hours before the phones start ringing and by 11am or so, you look at what you've done and it is substantial. Or at least it is an awful lot more substantial than if you'd started work at 10am. It's got to the stage now where if I've booked the day off because I'm working somewhere and it'll mean travelling times clash, I still start getting a bit edgy around 11am thinking that I haven't got enough done.

I should probably spend the £131 on a good psychiatrist but it's like pretty much everything else in this book. The time I spent looking into when I write the best has saved me more time later. Immeasurably so or I'd have measured it for you. It's also transformed me a bit: except when deadlines dictate otherwise, a standard pattern weekday for me now includes a relaxed hour from 2pm to 3pm as I go over what I've done that day and what remains to be sorted. If I sort it all, I stop working.

That's such a weird thing for me to say. Especially as I work from home and so there has always been the temptation to just nip back into my office to do this one quick thing.

And now, quite often, I'll read or I'll even cook. I'll go have a coffee with a friend who is either a writer too or has some weird working schedule that means they can be out knocking back the caffeine in the middle of the afternoon.

I'm starting to sound like I live in Brightsiding, Idyllicshire. Let's instead look at where you live: in this place where you get distracted easily, where the internet is not your friend, and when you have all this expensive computer equipment and you cannot find a thing two minutes after you wrote it.

It's time to look at *The Curse of You.*

Section 4

The curse of you

Ah, you're not so bad. You could do with being a bit more productive. A little sun wouldn't hurt. But if you have any fault at all, you know in your heart of hearts that it's just how easily you can get distracted.

You do also prevaricate quite a bit. If you put your mind to it, you can put off any writing at all, whether it's the long-planned novel or the piece an editor is phoning you up about and you promised yesterday. We're all like that but this section isn't for all of us, it's specifically for you.

In its chapters, you'll learn how to get started when you don't want to, when you've no idea what to do but you know both that the deadline is coming and that there's a really good TED Talk video online.

Want a quick-and-easy-to-say but quite-hard-yet-worth-it productivity tip? Learn to touch-type. I promise you, it changes the world.

Chapter 7

Figure yourself out

Some people like To Do lists, some prefer calendars. But while you can buckle each of them to sort-of, kinda, a-bit do the work of the other, don't.

That could be the whole chapter: don't.

You have to have a calendar so it's handy that you've already got one. But you can make it work harder, you can make entering events enormously faster and you can use it better with your To Do app, your email and your phone too.

Many or probably even most calendars on computers let you include To Do tasks as well as appointments. It's up to you but I'd rather you didn't. You end up using your calendar for all of your tasks and it simply isn't good or powerful enough. Plus, it literally ties your tasks to certain dates and you already know that's your ticket to a heart attack at the end of every single day.

Alternatively, you can be tempted to start putting some tasks in your calendar and some in a To Do app and that way begins with a certain amount of sanity but ends in an overwhelming amount of madness. You start putting things in that are really obvious like that phone call to the Mormon Tabernacle Choir that you said you'd do on Thursday, that'd go in to your calendar easily. But the MTC is a busy bunch, if you're not to waste the call, you need to plan what you're going to ask them and when exactly do you put that in your calendar?

Maybe you pick a date for that and go into this cycle of moving the task to tomorrow and tomorrow and tomorrow until you end up doing it right before the call. Or you put the planning into your To Do app and then you are stuffed. If you look at the To Do app, it doesn't tell you when the call is due. If you look in your calendar, it doesn't tell you whether or not you've finished the planning. Sooner or even sooner, you end up having to look in both and you end up having to keep looking in both. Over and over. And each time you think about whether this task in your calendar has an associated task in your To Do app, or vice versa, you're wasting time you could spend on doing this stuff. I'm more okay with wasting time than I sound but I'd rather waste it doing something I like.

Now, a To Do application that includes a calendar: that's different. Those I love. It seems such a simple thing, but to have my list of things I've got to do today followed by a stolen peek at my calendar is just great. It's everything I need to know in one glance.

I use my calendar for commitments that block out stretches of time: a phone interview that's going to take an hour, a day-long booking at a magazine. I do have birthdays on the calendar but mostly because I can't stop it. (I have an OmniFocus project devoted to birthdays and I use that instead. It tells me when the birthday is but also when I should start doing something about it. You can't believe how many people I know who have birthdays on the first of a month and knowing that this is the case, you can well believe how many times I used to turn the paper calendar over and go d'oh. I used to miss it on the calendar on my Mac too.)

David Allen in *Getting Things Done* calls calendar items like this the 'hard landscape' of the day. I like that term. I have no clue why. I can't bear the way he calls things you haven't done 'open loops' but I like the hard landscape. This is my week and month and year and here are the hills I have to work around.

Stop avoiding your calendar

Confession: my type of writing work usually lends itself more to To Do tasks than calendar items just because a given project might have a meeting at the start but the majority of the time will be spent writing and researching. It did get so that I wouldn't remember to even look at my calendar and that did cause problems. So while this may sound like a brute force approach, I have a repeating To Do task that is just "Check calendar for today and next week". I've weaned myself down from needing it every day to using it maybe twice a week, but it keeps my schedule in my head.

That would be enough of a reason to use my calendar: to make sure I don't miss an event or a work commitment. It's become something I refer to most days, chiefly through my To Do app OmniFocus. But there are ways to use your calendar more.

Using your calendar more and faster

You'd think that a calendar is a calendar and that whatever improvements could ever be made were done back when we switched from the Julian to the Gregorian one. But right now things are changing enough that I can tell you some ways to belt through adding events to your calendar and I can't guarantee that you'll be able to do it. Yet.

Your mileage will vary because your system does. But if your computer and your software calendar doesn't do this today, odds to onions it will tomorrow. These things are too handy not to be copied by every software maker in the world.

Actually, it's two things in particular. First, what's called natural language. It used to be that to enter an appointment with Susan for lunch next Friday at 2pm at the new Birmingham Library, I'd have to go to my calendar and then:

> Scroll to Friday
> Click to add a new event
> Drag to set it for an hour
> Type in that it was Lunch with Susan
> Type in the venue

It wasn't arduous. But it was a pain and if you were sorting out a lot of meetings, it was a right chore. Now I go to my calendar and I do this:

> Type "Lunch with Susan next Friday at 2pm at the new Birmingham Library"

That's it. No step 2. Where you actually type those words varies from software to software but in mine for instance – I just use the one that comes with Macs – there's a button with big plus sign on it. When I click that, it pops up a little box for me write this stuff in.

Once I've done that and hit Return, my calendar takes that line and parses it. It knows when next Friday is, I've told it the time, it reckons lunch is typically an hour, and I've told it the venue. I will often go in to extend or shorten the default length and I still check that it's right because I somehow feel this alchemy is too good to be true.

You think I'm mad to doubt it there, I can tell. Okay. How about this? The other day I was in a huge rush and even though I was at my computer working, I didn't have time to do any of this. But I knew I'd forget an appointment if I didn't do something, so I told Siri on my iPhone, I said aloud:

"Schedule a Skype call with Gilli for Sunday at 11am"

I'm going to tell you that I was a bit surprised when Siri asked me "Which Gilli?" but I reckoned it was just going to pull her full name from my address book. Can't fault it being thorough, I thought. So I told it.

Three hours later I needed to check something on my calendar. I hadn't done anything beyond talk to Siri on my iPhone, but you know the event was now in the calendar on my Mac. I knew it would be there. I trusted that it would be there and it was. What I had no idea would happen was that Siri would add the event to my calendar – and send an invitation to Gilli for it. But there it was: Gilli had received and had accepted the invitation so this event was now in her calendar as well as mine.

I don't get that many wow moments in computers and this was only half a wow, half an eeek. Because it had sent her an invitation to "Skype Call with Gilli Sunday at 11am". And at least once last year I'd scheduled an event I called Stupid Waste of Time Meeting that I Have to Go to. If I'd done this over Siri and if I'd said "Schedule the Stupid Waste of Time meeting with Bert that I Have to Go To", it would have invited Bert to it. With that event name.

So I'm a bit more careful with my event naming now. But I've used Siri a lot for this ever since and for the first time I really have found that speaking is faster than typing.

This is still this natural language idea: adding events to a calendar the way you would tell someone. It's just that now you can tell Siri or an equivalent.

It is funny how unnatural the term 'natural language' sounds. But if you dislike computer jargon, get a load of this: data detectors. You may never use the term in your life, but if your computer has these data detectors, you'll use them. Every day.

Follow. The majority of events I have to go to are meetings that someone else has arranged. Almost invariably, then, they will email me about it so

I'll regularly get messages like this:

> From: The President
> Subject: Vitally important meeting at the White House
> Date: 1 August 2013 06:44:55 BST
> To: William Gallagher
>
> William,
>
> The whole US economy is collapsing. I can tell you this because I trust you and because this is just an example email for a book's screenshot.
>
> What's important is that you be at the White House at 2pm on December 25.
>
> Can you make it?
> The President

If I see that on my iPhone, the part that says "at 2pm on December 25" is automatically underlined in blue, meaning I can tap on it to do something. On my Mac, moving my cursor over it shows me a dotted outline and a drop-down arrow. Tap on the iPhone or double-click on my Mac and I've entered an event in my calendar. It'll show me the event, it'll be one hour blocked out on Christmas Day from 2pm and the event will be the subject heading of the email.

I can change that, I can add a location, I can do all the things you might do when entering it from scratch. But all I usually do is look at where it shows me whether I'm already doing something that day or that time and if I'm not, I click once and it's added to my calendar.

This is called data detection because that email programme looks through all the text of your email, the data in it, for anything that looks like a date and time.

Then it's pulling all the relevant data that it can detect and is popping it into your calendar for you to go yay or nay.

So it's called data detection now but really soon it won't be called anything at all: it will just be the way that everyone does this because why wouldn't you?

Multiple calendars

This is going to get messy because I'm using the word calendar in two different ways. If you don't already, you soon will. My calendar, for instance, is the thing that shows me all the days that I am committed to something, it's the software I turn to on my Mac, it's the app on my phone. But you could choose to have many different calendars in one and sometimes you'll say calendar referring to them all, sometimes to the software, sometimes to just one of them.

Within any calendar software, you can make yourself a main calendar or you can add lots of different ones like a Work Calendar or a Leisure Calendar. Then when you add an event, you could decide that it should go in as work or as leisure.You could say it's a Writing Work one, it's a Sports Event Leisure one, you could go crazy with specifying everything. I've gone crazy. Or I did, anyway. I've now got – wait, I'll count them – 11 calendars in my calendar. They're not all my fault: one was automatically created by TripIt when I first had it add a train ride to my calendar.

Most of the rest are rubbish, most of the rest are from various attempts to get organised before I just got organised. I have a whole calendar devoted to events to do with one particular project that I now haven't touched in months. One, I now see, is to do with birthdays so in looking into this for you, I've finally discovered where to switch that off. Thanks.

This madness is easier to achieve than it sounds because it's really quick to create a new calendar. And if there are any used calendar salesmen and women in the world, what they would push on you is the whizzy way that you can make all these calendars and then switch them off. Before you think that's as daft as I think it is too, there is a logic here.

Say you have that Work and a Leisure calendar. You're looking at your week and it's pretty busy. Click a button, tap a box and you can hide the Leisure calendar. Bingo. All you're looking at is stuff for work. It's supposed to be incredibly useful and I suppose it does give you an idea of how booked up you are with high-level boardroom meetings. I can see why you'd do this within a company where other people can access your calendar to see if you're free. I get that one. You don't want to put "Interview with Rival Firm" in plain view.

But otherwise, I have truly no idea why you would do this. Maybe you block out Monday lunchtimes for a secret tryst with someone – I'm not judging – so, okay, then I could see you wanting to hide that away. Yet it's still there. Just because you can't see it, it hasn't gone away. So there you are with your secret tryst appointment or your job interview and you're asked if you can fit in an all-day Lego conference. Your calendar looks empty so you say yes and you'll think you're telling the truth.

But then when you turn to your calendar and actually try to enter the Lego conference, it will tell you no, you have a tryst meeting then. But you're off the phone by now and while I'm okay with looking stupid having to call people back to rearrange something I've got wrong, it is a ferocious waste of time. I think all of this is. Piddling about with multiple calendars, not knowing at a glance whether you're free or not, having to redo arrangements. I hate it.

So every single event I put into my calendar goes into the one calendar that I still use.

Except.

I have one more that I use. I just leave it permanently switched on and never hidden. It's a calendar I share with my wife Angela Gallagher.

Shared calendars

I don't want to know where Angela is. I need to know she's okay, but I don't want to know every pixel of her day. I'll ask her about it all before and afterwards, of course I'm very interested in all she's doing, but it feels stifling and maybe even just a bit creepy if I know all her appointments. It'd be like going through her handbag or something. Shudder.

But, nicely, a great many of those appointments will also involve me. And a huge number of things I do will involve her. So while we both have our separate calendars, we also share one.

Actually, I've not asked her whether she uses multiple calendars but I know that she has this one shared with me. When she enters an appointment or an event that I'm going to be at too, she puts it in a calendar called Angela/William. As soon as she does, it appears in my calendar too. When I want to add something for us, I put it in my Angela/William calendar and, wallop, it's in hers too.

Now, she doesn't know my calendar any more than I know hers so you'd expect there would be a lot of times when things clash. Surprisingly, not so much. I think most of the things we put in this shared calendar are theatre evenings and we tend to book those so far in advance that any one of them rarely clashes with anything else. But we don't get caught out with clashes because when one of us adds an event, the other gets a notification.

Actually, at the moment, we tend to get three and it's a bit irritating. I'd rather have three than none but I'll get an email, I'll get a push notification appear on my iPhone and when I next go in to my calendar, there'll be a little red badge saying I have an event I need to check.

Later, either Angela or I can change the times and date, we can add details like the address, and we both have the latest details all the time.

Notifications aside, this shared calendar is so useful that I'd call it mandatory: we use the bejaysus out of it.

I do know couples who share their entire calendar so that at a glance, each of them can see where the other is due to be. I understand it, I get that it means they know for certain that the other is free for a theatre event.

But for me, I'd much rather ask Angela how her day has been and what's coming up next than have it playing out on my screen.

Subscribe to calendars

One of my 11 calendars turned out to be a Bank Holidays one. I hate Bank Holidays, they're even worse than Sundays and the entire reason I didn't go in to banking for a career was so I could avoid having to take bank holidays. Nonetheless, somehow, I have them all on my calendar.

I could choose to have more things that are nothing to do with my work. Sports fixtures, for instance. Sport to me is as compost is to the space race but a lot of people like this stuff so a lot of people create sports calendars. Do a google search for the name of your favourite team or sport and then the word 'calendar' or '.ics' (with the dot). There are several ways to do calendars like this but the .ics format is common. I used this on my personal website, williamgallagher.com and its associated blog *Self Distract* (williamgallagher.blogspot.com) when I wanted to promote some events I was doing. You'd see the name of the event, a brief spiel about it and then a button. Click on the button and that was added to your calendar. I don't know how many people used it, but I did and it was handy enough that I'll do it again.

That was me plugging one single event at a time: I don't know how to give you one link that subscribes you to my entire public speaking schedule and lets me update it all the time, but then what are the odds that you would want this? It would be good to see you but you'd quickly tire of hearing the same types of event. Personally I think that's equally true for football as each game seems indistinguishable to me, but everybody else in the world disagrees and many teams have cracked this shared calendar lark so that you can subscribe to their events.

Write it once

The BBC used to do these great chunky diaries for its staff. I loved those. I think the last time I got one was in 2000; I'm pretty sure they stopped making them around then too. But up to the year 2001, I would get these diaries and I'd do the annual shuffle as I copied out all the repeating events like birthdays from the old diary into the new.

Or I'd mean to. In practice I think I rarely got around to it and each year's diary filled up with these things only as the days went by and I narrowly missed one calamity or another.

But perhaps because I'm wedded to this computer stuff and certainly because my handwriting is so deeply appalling – I once saw someone blanch when they got a form I'd filled in – but most definitely because I have no patience for unnecessary time wasting, I don't ever do this again. Not ever.

I don't think you're surprised at this but what I was surprised at was how much stuff in my life repeats every year. Usually when I add any event to my calendar, there is a part of my brain that wonders if this is going to come around again. So it's no great leap that when I think it might, I'll make that event an annually recurring one. There are commissioning rounds that tend to be at the same point each year, for instance. And certain points in the academic year that repeat a lot.

I'm still a bit mithered over these sorts of things and whether to put them in the calendar or not. Those commissioning rounds, for instance: this year I've put them in my To Do app as starting from a certain date. I think that makes sense because while I hope to get meetings to do with these rounds, all I know now is that I'll need to be ready and I'll write some ideas on that date. When I get a meeting about any of them, I'll add that to the calendar.

Reminders and alerts

Your calendar remembers events so you don't have to. Unfortunately, you have to. But you can use your computer to minimise the amount of stuff you carry in your head. Whichever system you use, your calendar will let you set a reminder alert for anything.

If you're a mathematician, you can set an alert for 4pm each workday that tells you it's time for tea. (If you're not one and so perhaps don't know this, professional mathematicians in the UK tend to stop at 4pm for a communal cup of tea and a natter. It's terribly civilised.) If you're the sort to miss anniversaries, pop the date into your calendar and set a series of alarms from one month before to one day before and you'll be fine.

Only, keep these to the very least you can.

If you don't, then the short term problem is that these keep popping up while you're working and you have to bat them away. Usually when you'd just got to a good bit in your writing

And the longer term problem is that you will then start to bat alarms away without even looking at them. They'll cease to inform or even alarm you and instead will just annoy. So you end up with regular annoyances, interrupted work and missed events. What's not to love?

I sound like I'm against alarms and notifications and so maybe even hanker for the days when I used to cart a typewriter around. But you know that writing is a lot easier now that we all have computers.

Still, back then in the olden days, like thousands and thousands of years ago, the blank page did stay blank until we filled it. Us. With our working. Now it is far too easy to fill that blank screen with – well, anything. Genuinely anything. Videos of cats. Everything. And we can and we do fill it instantly and constantly.

The internet is a tremendous thing and we must fight against it every day.

Chapter 8

The blank screen

Let me say this again: not a word of this book will improve your writing. The job of every pixel here is to get you more time to write.

But it is true that one thing guaranteed to soak up your writing time is staring at that blank screen with not one single clue what to write, how to write it, whether you've got any biscuits left, or why you ever wanted to do this stupid thing or ever imagined that you could do this sodding thing.

And that, I can help with.

I offer that actually we don't really spend all that long staring at a blank screen, it just feels like it because it's more in your face than most time-eating facets of our day.

There is perhaps one good or at least handy part to this blank screen paralysis, though, and it's that we generally have many different types of writing to do and some of it is so easy that I can tell you what to do.

Whereas for brand-new, tugged from your brain, bled over the keyboard creation that only you can do, I can give you just this:

> You have to walk around a lot of museums, a lot of sculpture parks. And time your caffeine, so that you are in an open, wide contemplative space for when the caffeine takes hold.
>
> (Singer/songwriter Dar Williams, interviewed in The Wall Street Journal. "The Queen of Banter Hits the Road" by Eben Shapiro, 12 April 2012)

I'm guessing she's talking about the judicious use of museum tea- and coffee-shops where I'm more a kettle kinda guy. If I could upgrade my kettle with new software every year, I would. Mind you, while I'm here wearing out the stairs carpet between my office and the kitchen, she's off writing songs. I wouldn't kill to write as well as Dar Williams does, but I'd maim.

You know that inextricably bound up with the brand-new, brain-tugged writing is the editing and the rewriting. You know about leaving your work for a few days so that you come back to it fresh, you know that sometimes the idea of having that spare few days to leave it is a laugh.

When this is the case, read something completely different.

There's a play called *The Westbridge* by Rachel De-lahay that I bought, once I'd heard enough of it to be sure I'd really enjoy it, specifically to be the thing I read in between two projects and clear my head of my stuff. That was months ago and I still haven't read it. Because something else came up that I had to do and it turns out that having to work on something else is fantastic for clearing your head of the original job. Then when you can physically come back to that, you're mentally ready for it too. Doubtlessly you're better off leaving your book for a year but when you've only got two hours, working on something else will do.

Get down to it

There comes a point when you can't put writing off any more, you can't read anything, there are no more biscuits, it's time.

Very often, that's great: you're ready and away off you go.

But sometimes, that blank screen looks awfully blank and the pressing deadline looks awfully likely to be missed. So do this: use these techniques to get started.

The *Bad Days* chapter talked about what you need to do when you're, well, not having the best time you've ever had. That will all help here too. But that was more for battling overwhelming workloads and demands on your time, here we're talking one single piece that you must do and that you want to do.

Start it. Write anything. There was a Charlie Brown cartoon where he wrote out the title "What I Did on My Summer Holiday" and then counted those words to see if he were any nearer the 100 he had to do for his school essay. Do that. Write down the title. Write down what the piece is supposed to be about. Just tell me: don't compose anything, don't think about it, just write down what you would say if I were there with you and a mug of tea.

You want me to say that out of this will come a better piece. I want to say that too. It might happen. I was always taught in BBC News that my job was "write to express, not to impress" and just telling someone something like it is does make writing better. It does make it express.

But coming to drama, I realised that expressing isn't anywhere near enough. Your writing has to express and move and persuade and seduce and tease and prick and upset and anger and tantalise and deny and lie its way to the truth. And it has to do it as only you can or we'd have no reason to read you instead of anyone else.

You won't get that on the page by writing "it's about this guy, right, and he does this thing that you won't believe".

Only, you're not writing this bit down for your reader or your audience, you're writing it down for you. Much as you write To Do tasks as if they're going to be done by someone else makes you be clearer about it, writing that kind of stuff helps you tell you what you're really after. Some writers find the one line that sums up the project and they plonk it in front of them for the whole time. I look for what something is about and then I look for what it's really about.

For instance, my very first *Doctor Who* radio drama, a short called *Doing Time* in 2010, was officially about the Doctor (Peter Davison) being in prison. It was really about this guy who is forever travelling, who is never stationary nor even pauses for breath anywhere, now being confined to one prison for a year. It had monsters and aliens and technobabble, all that, but this is what it was really about: how it felt to be the Doctor in prison.

I could've written this down and left it in front of me for the whole time. I could've written a paragraph about it at the top of the treatment or at the top of the script: I could've written it anywhere I liked so long as nobody else could see it and so long as I couldn't fail to see it all the time.

I didn't do that. Maybe because someone suggested this one-line lark after I'd finished the script – I suddenly think they were trying to tell me something – but also because I have been the sort of writer who dives in without a line and without a treatment in order to see where I end up.

At heart, I still am exactly that. I could ramble on and give you a spiel now about how much more liberated my writing is because I don't plan it all out in minute detail. And I could grumble as you point out that if

I outlined, I'd ramble a lot less. And I could confess that I planned *The Blank Screen* out a lot more than usual so that I could try getting you all this stuff in the quickest, clearest, least rambling way that I could.

But more than personal taste and what does or doesn't work for us, writers who outline have the very big advantage that they're never really starting from scratch. Not completely. An exploring writer like I have been will stare at that blinking cursor but an outlining writer can make a swift note about that bit toward the end where someone does something. It's effortless because it's just a note to yourself but it also gets something on the page.

I do believe that it is infinitely easier to change something on the screen than it is to make those first marks but I also think that it's quite a bit easier to make a second mark after you've made the first. So write down that line about the plot or what you're really after. Write down an outline if you like.

Write down utter rubbish if you need to. Start with nonsense poems, start with writing exercises that have nothing to do with your project. I fear sounding like a lecturer or, worse, like someone who is going to tell you all writing is valuable, that all your writing is great, and who hasn't twigged that we do this at least to reach other people, if not to reach them and make a living while we're doing it.

Nonetheless, writing down utter bollocks for five minutes is useful. Not valuable. But useful. It gets you going, it gets you something to change or replace or append and I think it also gets you deleting stuff. Before you start, that paralysing word count makes you want to count the title; after a bit, you're chucking stuff away all over the place and are writing stronger for it.

But, go on then, if anything you write down is useful to the process, let's have it out about outlines and whether they are the very most useful things of all. Or whether they kill.

The spiel about liberated writing

I said my heart was still a dive-in-and-explore sort. Right now, my head is less certain.

I've been using a thing called OmniOutliner – it's an outlining application for Mac and iPad by the same firm that makes the OmniFocus To Do app. I like OmniFocus so much that I checked out the firm's other offerings and tried this one because I came across it just as I was trying to work out a book project. That book was just so stupidly unwieldy that I couldn't see the words for the trees. With immense regret, I have to tell you that it worked. I've previously been an extremely reluctant outliner, only doing it when mandatory for a contract, and my heart is still not in outlining at all, but my head is. I realised this yesterday when I needed to figure out something else that I'd ordinarily have just got on with writing and exploring. And instead, I unthinkingly turned to OmniOutliner.

Here's the thing. Some writers plan out in immense detail, some don't. I fixed Alan Plater's email once when he was having trouble sending attachments and the example document that we batted back and forth in the process happened to be an outline. I didn't need to read it to fix the email, I couldn't read it because it was confidential, but I had to ask him. I had to. Why had he, of all people, written an outline? He told me to go ahead and just read it, I'd see.

It was a remarkably boring document. About as un-Plater-like as conceivable. But the very last line suddenly switched back into his voice as it went something like this: "Now can I just go write the bloody thing?"

Outlines don't kill writers, outlining does. We get the fun and worth of the story sucked out of us. Alan put it better in a memo to a producer – which I've got verbatim because it's in my own book about his show *The Beiderbecke Affair* – where he explained:

> This kind of story is in part a process of discovery and deduction for the writer as much as for anybody else. I know the A and the Z and have a reasonable knowledge of B to about K, after that it gets complicated and misty.

As I say, some outline and plan while others don't. My natural inclination is to explore on the page and I think I've been helped or encouraged in that as much by how well it's worked out and because I've written so much in magazines. Once I had the form in my head, once I knew how to write articles, I never planned again. Start at the top, write to the end, deliver. It's rarely quite like that but it can be and the number of changes I make are fairly few. Or they tend to be nuances and key points, they are never gigantic structural chunks being shuffled around.

Only

I could always see the shape of a piece in my head when it was a 5,000-word computer feature or especially when it was just a 70-word BBC Ceefax one. Books have proved to be somewhat harder: *Beiderbecke* was only 30,000 words or so but it was immensely hard to get everything in to that short limit. One of the books I'm doing now is 150,000 words and that defeated me: I could not hold all that in my head. Especially not when circumstances of when I could get certain research material, when I could speak to certain people, meant that I wrote about 100,000 of it completely out of sequence. I've asked the copy editor to please watch out for when I may have introduced someone in chapter 6 and then again when I got to write chapter 1. I think I've caught all that, but I have lain awake at night worrying about it.

That worry was from the sheer weight of words, the sheer volume of the volume. Drama is different. I have a big stage play on the go now and I can smell it, you know? I know the opening pages because I explored them, testing out the idea. And I know the very last line because, I promise, it will choke you up. I even know about eleventy-billion things that will happen, right down to entire exchanges of dialogue between these characters in my head, but the whole eludes me. That's partly because if it works, if I do this right, it will be the most delicate, gauzy writing I've ever done and the faintest breeze will wreck where I'm trying to take you.

I'm going to regret telling you that later when I've given up on the whole thing and turned to whisky. But could you outline something so fragile? If you could, do. Outline away.

I mean outline your own projects. Obviously.

Because

You can hear it in me that I am still an explorer. But you're not hearing me evangelise it the way you would have done a few years ago. You're not even seeing the kind of sniping I keep doing about Windows PCs.

And it's because there is a cost to exploring drama on the page. There is a price that I can't deny

I had heard a thousand writers extol and evangelise outlines and they were rubbish at it. All of them. Until one television writer said something like: "You can't have a blank screen on Tuesday night". He meant on your TV set, rather than on our word processors but it's another type of blank screen and it simply cannot be allowed to happen. It's just true. You can fight about what makes better drama, structured planning or freeform exploration, but you can't argue that when your job is to write a show that is airing, you have to write and produce something. A stunning work of piercing Tuesday night television drama is no use if the script is delivered on Wednesday morning.

It wasn't always like this. John Hopkins was commissioned over a pint at the BBC once in the 1960s and didn't deliver. Not on time. He wasn't especially pressed about it, though I understand the BBC did say, you know, how's it going, old chap? And then he turned in *Talking to a Stranger*, also known as the *Hopkins Quartet*. Four television plays set over the same weekend and all from the perspective of a different member of a family. I tell you, I read the scripts and when I reached the last one and realised why it was all done like this, why it wasn't just a gimmick, I cried.

If you want to tell me that Hopkins could do that from an outline, fine. If you even want to tell me that he did do it from an outline, fine. I have no idea either way. And that's the way it should be: whether outlines help or throttle a writer, it's the end result that matters, it's the audience that matters.

And whatever way you do it, no audience is ever going to see the rubbish you write down to get yourself going, they are never even going to see your first draft. Actually, if you're writing drama, they're never going to see your text at all.

But whatever you're writing, you are going to refine it and edit it and change it. Usually you want to, sometimes you're required to. But you're going to do it.

And this fact helps. It obviously helps the final piece but it also helps you with this blank screen business of struggling to get started. You may be doing something new, but the odds are that you've done something just a little bit relevant before. Maybe an email to a producer, maybe a five-year-old letter that has a germ of an idea you're now using in a novel. The note you made to yourself when you were cleaning the kitchen. Get any note, any text to do with any part of your idea and write that down.

So that you have started. So that you can change it. So you can make this a rewrite job.

Make it a rewrite job

This is easiest to cover with short documents like a pitch. You would never send the same pitch to more than one person. You would always aim it specifically at them, you'd always make sure you emphasised the right bits of your idea to most appeal to that person. But the idea is the same and if you can't re-use every syllable of the last time you pitched, you can use it as a first draft for the next one. You don't have to write a new proposal or pitch or outline from scratch, not if your sole purpose is to describe the project to someone else. If it isn't working or you're not happy or you have a better idea, then fine, go ahead and write your proposal or any document from scratch. But if it's just that you need to target someone else with the same idea, the perfect pitch you wrote last week is now the okay first draft for today's go.

And it's worth doing this because rewriting is easier. It is always easier to change something than it is to make those first little marks on the screen.

The only thing easier than rewriting is re-using exactly the same text again. And it is surprising just how often you can do that or really nearly do that. I've done it with scripts where I've changed the tiniest things and sent 'em off again. Can't remember why. And it hasn't noticeably benefited me or whatever the opposite of benefiting is. Whereas I've done this a lot with pitches and biographies and short form anythings – and they have benefited me tremendously.

Right now I've fallen a bit behind with this but I tend to keep three or four versions of my CV approximately up to date. If I'm talking to you about a script, you'll get the CV that puts *Doctor Who* and my stage work up at the top. If it's a book proposal, I show you the CV that has my television non-fiction books such as the British Film Institute's *BFI TV Classics: The Beiderbecke Affair*. You get the idea. I also keep a one-page, a half-page and a one-paragraph biography. If I were setting out today to write four CVs and three bios, I would feel like an egotist.

But because I wrote one CV and then later changed it because I was pitching to a book publisher, and because I wrote one bio when I was asked to for a book and then cut it down when a website wanted it, I have ended up with all these and I use them.

I've got a folder on Dropbox that contains all these different versions so wherever I am, whatever I'm doing and whomever I'm trying so very hard to impress, I can pluck the right document – and the right headshot photo or cover image – out of there and hand it straight over. I did a thing once where I and many other writers were asked to provide a bio and headshot; you know that I replied with both within a minute. You suspect that not everybody did. Most people took days, some took weeks, at least a couple took months. You know they spent more of that time dreading doing it than actually doing it. You know that I spent less than a minute thinking about it. And once it was gone, it was out of my head, off my list, forgotten.

In truth, it's rare that I can just wallop a pre-written bio over. I'm doing a short series of magazine pieces, for instance, where it would kill me to have exactly the same bio in each issue. So it's mostly the same but has a sentence that speaks directly to the point of the particular article in that issue.

Similarly, if I want to pitch an event or I'm invited to one and asked for a bio, I will start with the pre-written one that's nearest the length required, but I won't stop there. Usually I'll look at my CV, try to find two or three things that are related to the point of the event and then one that is crazily far away from it.

> William Gallagher has presented on writing topics at universities, taught writing to school age children and flown helicopters.

You know how hard it is to describe yourself, you know how very hard it is to write a bio but you can see how easy that paragraph was for me because I just plucked three things out of the CV. Didn't have to puff my-self up, didn't have to explain or justify or do anything but list the facts. I joined the first two because they looked like they belonged together and then threw in the one that was furthest away in topic that I could find.

Maybe I would send that, maybe I'd work on it some more, but of all types of writing, bios and the like are ones where it's much easier to change and improve than it is to start from scratch. So my method of starting might be mechanical, might be a bit soulless productivity engine-like, but it gets me started and then I can bring whatever writing skill or talent I might have and change it all.

The fact that I can concentrate on this changing or improving instead of on writing the first words also means that I will do it right away. Whether I do send that bio or I rewrite it some more, I will be working on it right now and I will be sending it right now. That's how I lobbed a bio and headshot over to someone before they realised they'd hit send on their email asking me.

I do like looking efficient, I admit it. And I really do enjoy freaking people out who are more used to writers squirming when asked how the work is going. But I can live without looking good. Being efficient with things like bios and proposals means that once I do them, they're done and I'm back to writing. That's the job, writing is the point of all we do, it's just that you also have to do all these other things. And if you can do some or even most of them faster, better, stronger, you get more time for the writing

Unless you truly do have a raging ego, though, you're unlikely to be ran-domly handing out bios and CVs every day so you're going to lose some time searching for the bleedin' things. Equally often, you'll need to look back at old scripts, old articles, old books and more often than it rains, you're going to have to look back across old emails. I was writing a scene the other day that I realised I'd done in a spec script 20 years ago; I found that script in a flat minute, saw why it hadn't been made but lifted the good bits because they fitted better in the new piece.

Strictly between, us, right, I also had a thing where an editor who didn't like my work had left to spend more time with his family. It took me longer to find out who his replacement was than it did to find an old proposal that I really wanted to do. I'll let you know how it works out, but even if it fails, it didn't take me much time because I found it all about as fast as I thought it.

Find things faster

You never need to search madly again. Promise. If you're on a PC with Windows 7, apparently all you need to look for is the search button on the taskbar at the foot. I say apparently because some Windows users prefer a thing called cygwin while others download Google Desktop to do their searching and presumably they have their reasons. And then there's Windows 8: I'm told that you're best off using the built-in File Explorer. Your mileage may vary, but so long as you've got some mileage, what matters is that you can get this stuff done.

On a Mac, incidentally, if you want to look up something, just look up. That magnifying glass in the top righthand corner of your menubar is called Spotlight and it is an excuse to be as disorganised as you like.

Click on that magnifying glass icon or tap Apple-Spacebar (I'm a writer, my fingers are on the keys all the live-long day, I tap that keystroke regularly) and then just start typing what you're looking for. If I didn't know what I'd called that proposal, I might begin by just typing a character name from it. I had a guy called Peregrine. Stands a chance that I'll find it with that name. If I've ever downloaded and kept a book on falconry that might pop up now, but probably the proposal will also be in there somewhere.

If not, maybe I remember that I changed Peregrine to Julius Blade-Feathering, so I'd try that.

Odd names are handy for this but even if you're the sort who likes rock-solid, ordinary names like Tom, Ahmed or Sarah, you're not stuffed yet. If a character name doesn't bring up the document you want or more likely it got you a huge long list of things to search through, just type a bit more. You can tell Spotlight that what you're looking for is a Word document created some time in 2005, featuring chocolate brownies, Doppler-shifted elephants and written under your pen name of Al Phabet.

It still might not find it, but if it doesn't, the odds are that it isn't on your computer. You've got backups, right? You've moved to a new machine but are still copying off the old bits, right?

Get it, got it, gone

So you've found your book, you've got your bio, your CV and your headshot. Put like that, it seems a lot and therefore it seems a lot of effort. But how many times have you not bothered to enter a writing contest because it's a bit of a faff? How long would it take you now?

Writing contests are great for getting you going toward a certain deadline on a new, spec project but they can also do double duty as excuses to contact people. Say you have an editor or a producer who you'd really like to work with and you keep trying with yet nothing quite catches. They're unlikely to be bowled over by your winning *Best Flash Fiction Featuring Coffee Contest* but winning that gives you a new excuse to contact them. You can see the worth of something simple like this:

> Hello,
>
> Just bursting to tell you: my play *Scorching Caffeine* just won the *Best Flash Fiction Featuring Coffee Contest.*
>
> Weirdly, I got the idea right after I spoke to you about dramatising the history of Yorkshire Tea. So thank you very much for putting me on this beverage theme.
>
> Al Phabet

So now you hear about a contest that fits something you remember writing in the Middle Ages, you use Spotlight to dredge it up, you give it a polish, send it off with your bio, CV and headshot, then forget about it and concentrate on your current work. If you win or get anywhere decent, immediately email every producer you still want to work with and tell them.

You've just become a writing contest engine, a publicist and a networker, and you've done it so fast you barely noticed.

Okay, you notice at first. But when you do this a few times, you start to stop noticing. It's not like I enter a lot of of competitions but I have had emails consoling me for having not quite won and, gosh, the standard was so very high this year, and it's taken me twice as long to remember what the contest was than it did to have entered it.

For all that I do this reusing of material, by the way, I never keep standard emails or letters ready. Never. Each email is specific and personal and built directly to do this one job of sending this one piece to that one person or company. I don't care that this is inefficient of me, I don't care that I probably unconsciously say the same or similar things every time – seriously, how many ways are there to say "here's a script"? – I will still never prepare standard emails. I don't want to be the kind of sales person whose focus and concentration and dedication is on the speed of turning deals over. I want to write and emails are where we writers can shine.

Don't underestimate the advantage you have in being a writer.

Productivity is an amazing thing but this is the perfect example of when you have to consciously remember that you're using it to do something, you're not doing productivity for its own sake. Spend that five minutes, that ten, that thirty to write a cracking three-line email because you can do that and so very many people can't.

I enjoy crafting those emails and the cold, hard commercial writer in me also likes doing this business of having bios and CV ready to go. It gets material out there, it stops me having to add more to my To Do list – because I've just gone ahead and done it right away – and it gets you noticed and remembered because it helps everyone. If you ever organise events or productions, you know that usually nobody replies until the last minute. And even though you know that, when you're the one organising the event you can't help but wonder whether they will or whether this time you've done something wrong and nobody will come. So a writer replying promptly tells you the invitations got out there, it tells you people are interested.

As the writer replying so promptly, you'll never get a prize just for being quick but I have had people give me my choice of dates for various things only because they are nice and because I was the first to reply.

Ultimately, it may be more important and useful to know that doing this kind of stuff actually does help with your writing – or that it can. Definitely no promises. But I do find that racing through things like this where I do have to be creative but I can have been that creative preparing material beforehand, it gets me going and ready for writing new material.

Even when it is just a tweaked bio and nothing to do with the current work, the fact that it's text on screen and that I have been working it, kneading it, somehow makes it that much easier to go on to creating something completely new.

It works for me, there's no way to guess if it will work for you, but give it a try. When you're paralysed over an idea, write something else. Write bios, write long emails, write rubbish. Give yourself the excuse to write that other thing, you know, the one that's on your mind and became instantly very important the moment you were commissioned for this one.

And accept that you're going to look up Facebook from time to time.

Chapter 9

Self distract

You don't need examples for this, you don't need to be warned that it might happen. It already does and you already do replace that glowing blank screen with Facebook. It's a funny world when the way we take a break from our screens is to watch our screens but it is a funny world.

Whether you do this in an office full time or overnight in your attic, ultimately writing is working for yourself: you have to do it and you have to beat the distractions.

Except when you don't.

If you're tempted away from your writing by Facebook or Twitter, fine. If it's actually LinkedIn that gets you hooked, well, er, fine. Google Plus. O-kay. If it's Myspace then we just don't understand each other. And if it's app.net then you've been invited and I haven't.

There is always another social media platform – I'm used to the word platform and still I don't like saying "social media platform' like it's a thing – and it's a thing. Some people tell you that you must banish it all forever and actually I'm going to go stand over in a corner with a few of those because I know you need to be able to switch it off. But then there are others who insist that you must use it and use it all, you must get out there and create a blog, promote your writing, sell, sell, sell, and them, I disagree with.

Here's why. If you go on to Twitter with a bit of an agenda on your shoulder, if you go on to Facebook solely to promote the latest interview you've done or the great whiz-bang special discount promo offer for your CD, I doubt I'll even notice you.

Why would I? Why should I? You're one of a million people doing this, I am another one of a million people doing it and just as it's not your job to read my tweets, it's not mine to read yours. I have to want to read what you write. Now, as it happens, that's very easy: if you write it, you personally, then I want to read it. But what about that writer next to you yesterday? I should read him or her too? If you recommended them, I would.

But here's that thing. Recommendation. People I have never met can recommend someone or something on Twitter and I am highly, highly likely to go take a look because I rate that person. Even without meeting them. And I rate them because I read them and because I enjoy reading them.

If they just came on to Twitter to promote their book, if that were solely what they did, the very most information I would see is that they have a book out. That's nice. I'd also take away an impression that they were only online to sell. That can be a harsh impression, it can be a quick one, but it's also very rapidly accurate. If I have seen them online promoting, I doubt I'll ever see them do it again because I will have gone.

Whereas, if a friend suddenly stops their usual nattering to say that he or she has a book out, frankly, I'll buy it. Right there and then if I can. I'll want to support them, I will be truly excited that they got this project away and I will share their news like mad.

This includes friends I've never met. People I've come to know over Twitter and Facebook – though I tend to only let in people I actually know in real life onto Facebook, some of them I got to know through Twitter – and whom I've never seen or might not even recognise if I did.

Every Friday, I write that blog of mine. It's called *Self Distract*, like this chapter, but it's not necessarily about productivity. It can be, but it's more about what we write and what we write with, when we get around to writing anyway. And when I've posted each entry, I will plug it on Twitter, Facebook, Google+ and LinkedIn.

I feel bad about doing it on Google+ because I don't live there. Right now I spend more time in Facebook than anywhere but for a couple of years Twitter was my thing, it was my spot at the bar. And I found it inexpressibly fantastic to be in a conversation at midnight. Ten of you, twenty of you, talking about nothing and everything and, yes, all in 140-character bursts. Such funny people, so warm, so joyous, and then you'd see a 21st person. You could feel them so gingerly throwing in a comment. You can just tell that they've been reading for hours, maybe in some cases entire weeks, and here they are taking that first little step into a teeming conversation. So you scoop them up, buy them a virtual drink and now you've got 21 people rabbiting on. Having a blast. There is nothing like it.

I'm sounding like an evangelist for Twitter and in fact I've fallen away from it, I've lost the delight of those midnight roars since I started the 5am starts. I miss them, I'll be honest. Not enough to burn candles but I do remember them fondly. Let's call it that.

So when I post about my blog on Twitter, I take some time to piddle about nattering to folk there and I do it because I enjoy it. I've lost the automatic habit of going on in between paragraphs of whatever I'm writing, but I'll go play in the park and I see it as exactly that, playing.

But as it happens, I can see the stats and I know when things happen. So I can see for certain that posting about my blog on Twitter gets me an immediate spike in the blog's readership where doing it on Google+ doesn't. Doubtlessly, there are online courses for how to improve your Google+ ranking or hit rate or whatever it's called, but I don't need them to know this: if you play where you promote, you will promote more.

Even that sounds terribly calculating. But, seriously, treat these things as your friends. If you ever go to Bert down the road to get your spanner back and you would tell him about your new commission, tell people on Twitter. The reason I am excited for your new CD is that you are excited. It's tremendous seeing someone happy, most especially a writer since we can be a right miserable bunch. But if I only ever see you when you're promoting, meh. If I only ever see you and you are constantly promoting and everything is ace, the world is golden for you, well, I'm going to be happy for quite some considerable time but there will come a point when I would like you to shuddup. And there are shuddup buttons on all of these things.

Go on Twitter, go on LinkedIn, have a ball. If there are going to be other benefits, then all of them will follow from you just enjoying yourself. And if there aren't any, you've still had a good time enjoying yourself. So it is great, it is nothing short of tremendous that you are tempted on to these things. The fact that you're tempted means you're going to enjoy it and there's nothing wrong with enjoying it.

Well, except for this distraction business. I just wanted to say first that social media is your friend, it isn't a tool – or it isn't only a tool, you shouldn't use it as just a tool – but it isn't your enemy. And the fact that it distracts you is potentially a good thing.

But there will come a time, there does come a point when you have to ignore the temptation and the distraction and get down to some writing.

Two answers, no waiting

There are broadly two things you can do to stop getting distracted by the internet when you need to concentrate. The first, and I think most useful, is a bit of a distillation of things you've already read here. Things such as all the ideas and advice in the *Bad Days* section: what helps you get and keep working then will help you now when your worst problem is an Angry Birds addiction.

But then there are brute-force solutions. Answers based on technology or on sheer will power. If we had will power, we wouldn't have a problem, we'd just write when we needed to and merrily ignore Twitter like the very efficient and very boring person we'd be. Let me dispense with the willpower answer by just pointing out that actually, yes, you can do that. You can choose to ignore any distractions while you work and you know you can because you know you have done. Remember all the times you wrote under pressure. No distractions then. And once you can get started on some writing, you're going to be okay. Not forever: you'll hit snags and that'll take some more effort but you've done it before, you'll do it again.

Technology solutions

Assuming that willpower is not an option, or at least that it's a rubbish option, then look at getting your computer to help you. Given that the number one distraction of all writers since Dickens is the internet, it's nicely ironic that your computer is in the perfect position to help you.

If you're on a Mac or PC, look at a tool called Freedom. It costs $10 (that's in US dollars because you can only get it from the developer in America; in the olden days that might've meant international money orders, the Post Office adding on an awful lot of charges and a lot of waiting, now it means one click on the Freedom website and your bank adding on an awful lot of charges for converting the currency for you). There are other applications that block your internet, but this one has been recommended to me by friends. Run this and from, say, 9am to 5pm, your internet won't work. No browsing, no email, no nothing. It is hell.

I don't like this type of software internet blocking and haven't used any of them, ever. So much of my work involves various checking details online or emailing folk, for ~~flimsy excuse~~ example. Adobe Creative Cloud gets cranky if you don't have an internet connection too. I'm a writer, clearly I need to spend hours in Adobe Photoshop at any given moment.

You can't get much cheaper than $10 for saving your mind, soul and concentration but you could be clever and ask your friends online to help you. Tell them straight, you're working and if they see you tweet or post, they should scowl at you. It works, especially if you help them in return.

I'm sorry to sound calculating again, but doing that also helps you appear to be busy when you need to appear to be busy. There are so many times when the only way to write is to walk away from the keyboard but if you have clearly stated on Facebook that you're writing today and then you don't go back on for hours, you certainly look busy. That's nice for you. But when your editors and your producers and your cast and your directors have become your friends because you like them and because you have no social circle outside work of course you've got them on Facebook and then it doesn't hurt that they see you're busy and can assume it's on material for them.

Mind you, if you have some crazy moral objection to being an utter lying bastard all the live-long day, you don't have to do this online, you don't have to claim to be busy, you don't have to claim that you're going offline. You could just pull the plug for free. Close down your email, switch off your internet connection. Take your laptop or iPad or paper-and-pen to somewhere without wifi. That's easier with pen and paper but you can manage it whatever you write on. And also wherever you write.

This is nudging toward me attempting sage writing advice rather than the straight practical productivity I promised, but location matters. For some reason when I was working on two rather different books at the same time, I got into a habit of writing one in my office and the other in my living room. I came to associate the books with their rooms: not to the extent that I'd talk to my editors about the office book, but to the extent that it cleared my head. When I'd be writing in the office for a few hours, I'd take a break and go to the living room to work on the other book. One day I was also writing a script in the kitchen, but you can go too far.

Every writer is different so you may need to be Sellotaped to a particular place or you might be the type who can plonk anywhere and write anything. I actually thought I was the latter, though, and I am definitely used to writing in stolen moments while travelling. But even for me, the complete change of location and machine – I had a MacBook in the living room and made sure it had no files on it to do with the office work – made a big difference.

It certainly made a difference to the quantity of work I got through and I was writing with the awareness that I was going to have to revise and improve the text a lot, but I was fine with that. In the end, however, I'd come back to revise the main text and wouldn't be able to tell what I'd written when. Plainly, I may be rubbish, but I'm consistently rubbish.

Whether you will or won't benefit from changing locations to work on something else, try to just do work at your desk or your computer. I'll be there at my desk for six hours straight and I'll relax by eating lunch in front of a film on the same computer. It is a gorgeous screen, it's actually substantially better than my TV set, but GO AWAY FROM THE SCREEN.

Even, whisper it, go for a walk.

Change something

If you can't swan off to another room to work on something else – because you're in an office, because you have kids using every available inch of floorspace, because there is physically no time to leave your desk – try changing something else.

And try using some of the ideas you've already read here. Specifically, change your email to only check for new messages every hour.. That's a gorgeous one. Remember to get your phone to do the same or you'll still be hearing that bleep that beckons you like a siren call.

Whatever you're doing, finish it. Promise yourself that you won't do anything else until you finish that email, finish that paragraph, that scene, anything. You can't easily say how much it is you'll need to finish, it's not always as obvious as one email or one scene, but you do always know exactly what it is that you burn to run away from. So don't. Promise yourself that you will stick with that one thing and not look at anything else.

And if you struggle with that or you get interruptions you simply cannot ignore, try ignoring them just a little bit. No matter how many calls, emails or notifications you hear or see coming in, tell yourself that you will ignore them to the top of the hour. Whether it's now two minutes after the hour or forty-five, swear to yourself that you won't look or respond or react to any of these interruptions until the hour is up. Quite depressingly, when you do then look you're going to find that you didn't miss much. It's more fun when you think you're having to respond urgently to so many things, but making them wait is fine for them and better for you. Dealing with them at 16:00 instead of 15:45 didn't make a big difference to whoever was emailing or calling you. Whereas not stopping or pausing or leaving your writing between 15:00 and 16:00 makes a very big difference to you and your work.

This is setting a time when you'll deal with something and that's another sort of deadline. It's very easy to say that a deadline focuses the mind but you know it doesn't really. There does come a time when that deadline is so close that your eyes water and your stomach cramps up yet still you long to be doing something else. That's a really important email you've got to read. If I don't write this idea down, I'll forget it. I deserve a tea break. I've earned a biscuit. All true. Mostly. Sort of.

Only, that email actually will wait. If you do forget that idea, it's fine, let it go. Call me positive or negative here, but if you forget the idea, forget it thoroughly and you'll then also forget that you forgot it. What you've forgotten that you've forgotten can't bother you. If you want a nicer point, it's that you'll have that idea again or you'll have many others and in the end the ideas don't matter unless you do something with them. And you're doing something with a previous idea right now.

You don't deserve a tea break, sorry. You haven't earned a biscuit. But in one hour, just sixty minutes, by God you'll have earned it by then and it will be the sweeter for it. In the end, the work is the reward.

And before you throw something at me for that, let's get back to that important email and do some specific and particular things that will make email useful again.

Chapter 10

Make email useful again

You open your email first thing in the morning – if you haven't already checked it on your phone – and you close it again at night. If you ever close it. In between, it is your one biggest repository of all information ever and it is also your one biggest interruption.

And sooner or later, it's going to be your biggest problem because you're going to email the wrong thing to the very worst of the wrong people. But you can reduce the odds of that and you can make this all actually useful once more instead of overwhelming.

Perhaps this isn't a thing any more, but it used to be that getting letters through the post was quite exciting. You had to be young and it had to be one of your first times, but we were all young and we did all have first times. Somehow, though, we went from wanting the post to dreading it. Maybe you play the game *So How Long Did One-Day First Class Take This Time?* Maybe you open your post standing right over the shredder and the recycle bin. But you no longer look forward to it.

The same thing happened to email. There is still a little bit of a thrill when the name of someone you rather like and hope they rather like you appears on an email. Especially when they've emailed you, but even when they're just on the CC list. But other than that, email is now something you have to do and to deal with rather than something you enjoy.

Nothing will make it exciting again. But plenty of things will make it significantly easier to cope with and doing those will make you want to use it more.

There are, what, three problems with email? Number one has to be the sheer volume of it – which fills you with dread, clogs up your ability to get attachments and also makes it impossible to find anything. But then there's the fact that everybody emails you expecting answers but nobody bloody replies when you need something.

And we'll treat this separately because the solution is different, there is also the fact that sheer volume of emails from the demanding people keeps pinging in to your mailbox every few seconds and thereby destroying any chance of you focusing on anything else.

The toughest one to crack is the volume, so let's deal with that right now.

At this minute, you probably have eleventy-billion emails in your inbox.

You leave a lot of those there because you'll need them someday – a fiver says you never will, but still – and then you keep a lot around because they're like your To Do list. Or they used to be. You're better than that now. You're cured.

But even without these, there are still all the unread ones. You probably did glance at the three- or four-line preview and decide you didn't have to read further but you left it there so that counts as unread and keeps that total high.

Deal with it

Just do this for the very next email that comes in. Only the next one.

Read it and decide which of these the message is:

Spam
Something you need to know
A request
Something you have to do
Reference material to read
Natter from friends or colleagues
Details of some future event you might like

You can think of other categories but whatever they are, they really come in one of three sizes:

Do it
File it
Delete it

By volume, most emails you get in the day should be deleted. So delete them. It comes in, you see it's spam or junk or in some way not of use to you, and you delete it right away. It's gone and you never have to think about it again. Face it: they're going to send you the same junk again tomorrow anyway. And if there's something in there that you think maybe one day you might just want to know a bit more, then one day you'll go looking for it out there in the wide world. You won't look it up in that email because you'll have either forgotten about the thing or, most certainly, forgotten about the email. Keeping it doesn't help you later.

Keeping it does clog you up now. If it's junk or spam or a newsletter or anything that you didn't positively ask for today and doesn't have something in it that you want right now, this minute, then kill it and never look back.

The Do It sort has two flavours. A lot of times the thing you're asked to do or that you reckon you ought to do because of this email will take you a minute. Maybe five. Nothing more. So just do it. Don't bother putting it as a task on your To Do list, just do it and it's done.

There will be others where you're going to have to spend a lot more time. I have a mailbox called Follow Up which I am unfortunately poor at working through but I'm getting there. Anything I can't dispense with right away goes in there and, actually, if it's that important, I'll probably also add it to my To Do list. But that's partly because the software I use is helpful with that: I can forward an email right into my To Do list. Oh, that is so good. And it's OmniFocus. Did I mention that before?

So if you do this as each email comes in, after a time you will have deleted a pile of them, you've done a pile and you're going to do a pile more. Just chuck the rest, all the old ones into your archive. Every mail system has an archive and some are handier than others: sometimes you can be reading an email and just tap a button to file it away. Sometimes you have to drag it into an archive folder. Just sometimes, your email doesn't have an archive folder so you need to create one. But then you tap or you drag and it's done.

The minimalist in me rankles at the thought of chucking it all into an archive when you can be certain you're saving junk and spam right alongside the good stuff. But otherwise, this is really what I recommend. Take it all, shove it away, and you can forget about it.

But there are a couple of things about this. One is that you're thinking you will be ignoring important stuff. You will, but:

> If it's that important, you'll have already added it to your To Do list

That's probably not true yet if you're just getting organised but it will become true and moreover:

A fiver says you'll never need this stuff again anyway

And:

If you do, it'll be because someone asked you about it

Which means so long as you can find it again, you're fine. And these days, email is smart enough that you can find it.

So I'm telling you that you must clear out your inbox because it is too full and you can't find anything – but what you should do is bung it all into an archive mailbox where there'll be millions of emails but you can find them all easily.

Yep.

Your main inbox is special. It's the one that changes most often, it's the one you read most often and it's also the one that is available to you on all of your machines and devices no matter what system you use. Some systems keep all emails available always, others store older archive messages on one machine and hope that you back that computer up.

But for me, it's the fact that you read your inbox the most that makes this important. Just as with churning over a To Do list of things you can't do yet, so reading and re-reading that inbox takes up your time and takes up your concentration when you could be writing. If nothing else, Do, File or Delete is quick.

The root of this whole idea is that you shouldn't need to think about a particular email more than once. It won't happen: you have to work through your Follow Up mailbox and think about the ones in there each time. But the closest you can get to seeing once and dealing with it, the better. Truly.

Less of your head is taken up fretting this stuff, for one thing. Because you now do so many things as soon as they come in, you get a reputation for being efficient and productive – and you feel efficient and productive. Because you are. So many of our tasks overwhelm us just because there are so many of them. Any individual one can be tiny, so deal with it before it gets added to the morass of other tasks weighing you down.

There is a risk that if you do something immediately and reply immediately that you will then immediately get another email back. I am very bad at this: I will get into lightning fast email exchanges with someone and enjoy it very much but it's sapping my time and I feel awful for how it's doubtlessly sapping theirs. Sometimes I will put an email into Follow Up and leave it an hour just to make sure I won't get into instant email tennis about it.

Other than that potential pitfall, this is all good. And it's got a name: Merlin Mann calls it Inbox Zero. So do a lot of people but I think it came from him first. Maybe Merlin Mann with a dash of David Allen.

But it's called Inbox Zero because you end up with absolutely no emails in your inbox. While I've been writing to you now, I've seen my iPhone screen flash some notifications and I'll bet money that there is now a handful of emails for me to answer. So right now, this moment, my inbox is not zero.

It will be. When we're done here, I'll work that inbox and I will decide on the spot whether to do, file or delete them.

I really don't like this Do, File, Delete business: I mean, I like doing it and it has helped me, it's just the name I don't like. I feel as if I'm trying to make up jargon. Sorry about that.

I will tell you that the first time you achieve this – and it is an achievement, it feels like one and it is one – then you'll look at your completely empty inbox and it will feel wrong. Just wrong. Give it a little while, though, and suddenly the reverse is true: it feels wrong when there is any email in that inbox. Even now, I should've turned my phone over or off because I'm aware there are some emails and it's making me itch.

There are archives and there are archives

So far, I've used the word archive to mean some mailbox other than your inbox, one that you will dump all email into when you're finished with it. The trouble is, email adds up. That's actually another reason to get it out of your inbox: when you have 10,000 emails in there, everything slows down every time you try to read one or scroll back a few. When you've got 20,000 in your archive, well, it's probably the same but you just never scroll back and you're hardly ever in there so you don't notice.

At some point, though, enough is enough. Gmail insists that you will never have to delete an email again so if that's true and it's true for you, skip on. But for most systems, there is some limit. Not an actual, physical, one-more-email-will-break-it limit, but a practical limit where everything has slowed down and it takes you longer to find things. You'll need to get rid of some. Or, more realistically, do the other type of archiving: saving this stuff to somewhere safe and then deleting it from your Mail.

You don't want to do this. But eventually, you'll need to. The biggest thing against it, for me, is that once stuff is sent out to this Proper Archive and is off your Mail system, it's off your Mail system. You can't get to it without a bit of effort. You can't, for instance, be on your iPhone running for a plane and needing something you know you had emailed to you in 2005.

But iPhones use iCloud, by default, and at some point either the stuff is not going to be on your iCloud space because you've chosen to archive it off or it won't be there because you can't afford to keep buying more iCloud space just to hold emails from a decade ago.

This is getting picky and it's also getting a bit too specific: your Mail system is probably different to mine so either of us saying which button to press first is going to drive us mad. (An aside. The single most irritating thing I have ever read is *MITE for Morons* by Arthur C. Clarke. It's included as padding in the back of his book with Peter Hyams about The Making of 2010. This was the 1980s and Clarke said, frankly, get used to it: email is the way of the future. He gets points for that but he later loses them for apparently deciding that fax was better still. Tell that to the poor sod who had to retype out *3001: A Dreadful Odyssey* from fading fax paper. And Clarke for me loses all points forever because after saying this about email being the future, he said that we're going to have to learn how to use this stuff sooner or later so here it is. Here is how to use MITE, the email system he used. It's not like he invented this thing, it just happens to be the one he bought. Perhaps he just copied out the manual, I don't know, but for the next few pages we get line-by-line and button-by-button instructions on how to work his email software.

If I'd had the patience and the nerve and his address, I'd have emailed him similar notes detailing the one I happened to use then. Cix for Eejits, I'd have called it.)

Anyway.

It's most likely that I just don't know how to use your system. If I had a go at it here, I'd have to show you seven of the buggers and still I might miss yours. So let me summarise all of them:

Export your very old email

There will be an Export or a Share option. It'll be there. If you don't know it, can't see it and Google isn't helping, email me at william@the-blankscreen.co.uk, tell me what you use and I'll try to work it out for you.

Wherever it is, it'll give you some way of saying you want to archive off all emails older than five years or something. I keep a few years around but it's up to you. The hard fact is that if you archive something off, it'll take you longer to get it back later. But the harder fact is that you're never going to want it back. I must have emails going back to the 1990s and I haven't looked at them since the 1990s.

So I'm not sure why I even keep them in these backup archives but I do and at least they're off my main email system. For me, that means I'm paying less in live online storage and it means my mail program is faster. But it's a personal choice how much or whether you archive and while I want to urge you to do it, I also want to skip on because you can do all this any time. As important as it can be some day, today you need to be getting more productive with the email you've got that needs your attention. So let's continue with that and also examine the apparent mixed messages I've been giving you. Specifically, the advice where I say empty your inbox but fill up your archive. This is true. And it's not conflicting.

Because of how the inbox is special and the archive is not. While you're reading your inbox every single time you go into email, you rarely read the archive. Let it pile up. Because you can get your computer to search it.

Seek-Locate-Emails

The headline answer here is that whatever computer you've got, you can use it to search for emails you've written or received. Some make it easier than others, that's about the strength of it. Have a squidge down here until you hit something that applies to you. Then we'll get on to the basics of using it all so that you can forget the computer stuff and concentrate on your real work.

PCs and Windows

If you're on a PC, apparently you can use Windows Search to dig into your email.

I say apparently because here's the thing. If you are a Windows user and you ask Mac fans what you need to do to get some particular Mac-like feature, they will all answer "Buy a Mac". If you are a Mac user and you ask Windows fans the opposite question, you get a lot of answers and they divide into four types. One will be incredibly technical. One will be that you need to buy some extra particular application or other. The third will be that OF COURSE you can already do that in Windows and of course IT IS MUCH BETTER. Then the last response won't actually be an answer, it will be an accusation that you are stupid for wanting to do that.

Including the unhelpful Mac fan's answer, that's five guaranteed responses to anything you want to know. Five that don't help, five that make you wish you hadn't asked.

It's as if the only way to find out what you want to know is become the expert you wish you could ask. I have no clue how you do that without asking questions. What I can tell you is that I know this stuff pretty well for Macs and you can ask me anything.

Back to the plot.

Windows 7 has Windows Search. With Windows 8 it's similar, but you have to be in Mail to search your email. I suspect Microsoft would tell you that this is to make it simpler. I suspect they're right – but simpler for its programming staff, not for anyone using the thing in the real world.

Gmail

You can use Google's Gmail just about anywhere: PCs, Macs, iPhones, Android. Wherever you use it, things may vary a bit but core mail.google.com service will always let you search for anything. It's email by Google. Of course it's searchable.

Android

The big advantage of Android is that it's great for people who like to customise the bejaysus out of their phone. People who don't like to be told to work one way, who just want to know their phone can do these things and they'll set it all up the way they want. Your Android phone can do these things, they're over there somewhere, you knock yourself out. (Translation: I tried to find out how to search your email on an Android phone and I am still wide-eyed at how many versions there are even for the basic things.)

iOS for iPhone and iPad

In contrast to Gmail and Android, I may prefer iPhone and iPad in everyday use but just they aren't great for this. With Apple's gear, right up to iOS 7 in late 2013, you had to go into your archive or your Follow Up mailbox and search for an email there. You couldn't just search across all of them. Worse, you could only search the subject heading or the names of the people sending and receiving the message. If you don't find it in Follow Up, you had to go to the archive and search again there. If you were looking for a document, you have to go to the app that created it.

This has all improved somewhat and it gets better again with iOS 7 but it's still a chore.

Which is odd because Apple's other device, the Mac, has an email search system to crave.

Mac

Now this, I love. Because it's Spotlight. Yes, I can search for any emails I like but I can chuck anything into mail, into my documents archive, Dropbox, anything, anywhere, anywhen. Because at any time I like I can then tap two buttons and tell my Mac to search for something and know that it will look across emails, documents, web pages, everything, until it finds it. And it finds things very fast.

And the point is

Back in the olden days, if we were organised at all, we used to have email folders for family emails, folders for work, folders for emails to do with the book we're writing. Now computers are so fast and searching can be so good that the time it takes you to be organised like this does not save you any time later.

I can get a notion now to find all the emails I ever sent Bert which mention both Amy and the police, have an attached arrest report, have the subject heading Pineapple Ransom, and that were CCd to her community care officer. If I had a Bert folder with a chain of subfolders for Amy, police, pineapple, ransom it would still be faster to use Spotlight to find the one I wanted. And all the time that you spend deciding you need a Bert folder and havering over whether to have one for all emails about Amy or just the ones where she got convicted again, that's time you could have spent writing.

Or eating ice cream. What you do with your time is up to you and you may well like having folders but overall, I recommend ice cream.

For the record, what I'm saying is that you should have the Inbox that comes with your mail application and then three other folders named something like Follow Up, Hold and Archive. You can see what they're all for. If you're not sure about any of them, it's Hold. What I'm saying is that once you've read an email, bung it in Hold if you're going to need it over the next day or two. Like a dispatch confirmation email that includes a link to a tracking service. That kind of thing.

I'm saying Follow Up is for stuff that you can't reply to quickly and immediately but will get to soon and must get to sooner. And everything else, everything else goes into Archive.

That's what I'm saying. What I'm doing is almost the same.

Right now I have six mailboxes on all my devices:

Inbox
Follow Up
Hold
Archive
Travel bits
Ancient stuff

You know the first four. The very last one is where I've left all the emails since before I began to use this Inbox Zero thing. My plan was to work through those a few emails at a time until I had dealt with them, deleted them or archived 'em but, you know, Spotlight searches that folder just as fast as it does anything else. I should really drag the entire lot into Archive. I think I will. Thanks.

But first, let me tell you that my Travel bits mailbox is where I drag all ticket emails for trains and coaches and planes. I use TripIt for iPhone whereby you just forward these emails to a special address and all the details get added to the TripIt service and pop up nicely on your iPhone. But some operators I travel with look at me very suspiciously until I show them the same information in their own email layout. And TripIt is an American service; it's doubtlessly hot on all US travel operators but it falls over on some UK ones I use. Most of the time, it's a great service and if I can't always wave TripIt at a coach driver, I can always use it to look up when I'm next supposed to be where.

I have all this gear, you have all this gear, we should and we can use it to make stuff quicker and easier. So it'd be pretty good if we could get our own computers to do some of this deal/delete/archive work for us. And we can. Via Email Rules.

Email rules OK or at least OK-ish

Windows and non-Apple software seem to do email rules better. I don't know why: I think it's an issue with iCloud but that's a moving target so all I really know is that it's been an issue for me. Enough so that I've scaled back the number of automatic email rules I've set up and I usually just do things manually.

If you don't know yet what an email rule is, I don't think your heart is bleeding for me. But let me give you an example. Yesterday I bought a train ticket online and the firm emailed the ticket to me. I ought to be able to tell Mac OS X Mail that whenever it gets an email from this train company, forward it to my account on that TripIt service.

I actually do have a rule that does this, yet it doesn't always do it. So yesterday I manually forwarded that ticket email to TripIt. Fine. Only, for some reason my rule worked too. Just this once. No idea why. It bugs me, but I reckon it's better to have two copies of the ticket than none so it's a background bug rather than something I'll deal with.

However, if you rely on services such as Gmail or Outlook, you've got rules and they usually work very well. I can't tell you the specifics of click here, tap there because every email application is different but this is the kind of thing you can do:

> Any email from Bert, reply with "I'm not paying any more bail money" and delete the message so I never see it
>
> Delete any email from TripIt with a subject that begins "TripIt Itinerary Ready for" [because it's just a confirmation that the service worked; I only need to see when it doesn't and those emails have a different subject heading]
>
> Any email from these seven people with a subject ending "{URGENT}" forward to these four other people
>
> If the email is from Sally Decker and says the words "booking" anywhere in the message, send a copy to my Evernote notebook Events.

You can get very creative with this stuff – and you've already done so. Or at least you've already seen other people do it. You know those out-of-office autoreplies you've probably set up and unquestionably received myriad times? They're done with an email rule. It's either:

> Reply to any email with the following message

or

> If the email is from that writer, then send an out-of-office reply whether I'm gone or not

I cannot remember the last time I set an out-of-office rule. I'd believe you if you said it wasn't since 2007 when I got an iPhone and brought my office with me. But I just looked and I do have an out-of-office automatic reply. It reads:

> Is this thing on? I don't do holidays, I've not tried this before. Testing. Testing. Hello. If you get this, I'm away from my office until Tuesday 23 October and will reply to you then. If you don't get this, I'll still be away and I'll still reply to you then, but you won't half be ratty by the time I finally pop up. William

Maybe I haven't used it in a long time – I know for certain that this particular 23 October was not last year's one – but generally speaking, out-of-office is so commonly used that it tends to be treated differently to other rules. Your email client might have a section specifically called Out of Office or Vacation where you can write some of your own standard buck-passing text and have a great big On/Off button. It's still an email rule and whatever your system, you could set it up wherever good email rules are sold.

If you don't know where your email keeps its rules, you could look for sections called Tools or Preferences. But I'd Google it.

So much for searching

You can now find emails faster, you can deal with them quicker with rules, you can stop worrying about where that particular message is and you can go crazy searching for Bert's ransom notes. But even though you will always get many millions of times more emails than you send, you've got to send a fair few too.

I really don't believe in pre-baked emails that you write once and send a hundred times to a thousand people. If you weren't a writer, I'd say okay, write it once and forget it: writing's hard enough without making yourself go through it again and again But as you're a writer, I'd say go through it again and again. Each time you compose an email to someone, you are using your skills to communicate to that one specific person – and it doesn't hurt that you're also therefore advertising that you can write.

But it's up to you. And I do bend my rule for emails that are strictly formatted: there's one financial email I send regularly where all that changes is the pile of figures in it. So I use a thing whereby I type a certain three-letter code and it addresses the email correctly, pops in the right subject heading and then asks me for the figures before dropping them into the form. I use TextExpander for that. It's the same software I use for my *Shape of the Day* and Daily Log escapades.

Otherwise, let's write everything new. And if you're now wondering what I could possibly have to tell you about writing emails, I'm afraid the answer is a lot.

First, let's do some straight, ordinary technical stuff that people tend to forget and so either end up sending a very private, personal email to a million people or telling each of those million the email address of the other 999,999. But then how to write emails that just do their job faster: that help people reply to you sooner and with what you need from them.

Reply to All and Groups

To email one person, write their name in the To: bit of the email. Doddle. To email two, write them both in there. Also a doddle. When it gets to be ten people and you're emailing them all with something new every few days, make a group. You'll need to check your email's help screen for how to do this, as it varies so much, but once it's done, you'll just type a name or phrase like Banana Splits Fan Club into the To: and your email programme will pop in all ten addresses for you.

Just be certain you want to email them all.

You're not likely to make the mistake of sending to everyone by accident when you're writing a new email but you can well make it when you're replying. Get into the habit of hitting Reply and never, ever Reply to All. Many times you're going to curse and think what a pain it is that you've got to close your reply and do it again as a Reply to All, but that's somewhat better than cursing after you've sent the wrong email to the worst group.

I was once in a firm where a colleague was doing a PhD, I think, and wanted help from everyone. She emailed everybody a questionnaire about their lives, their work, where they saw themselves in five years, all that. And of about 120 people, I think 40 did Reply to All. I shouldn't have read their replies but they were right there and it was wincing how many had admitted to her, 'privately', that they were intending to leave this wretched place as soon as they could.

If you think you'd never do that, think again: this firm was a computer magazine. These people should've known what they were doing.

Similarly, I was once one of a group invited to a particular drinks party organised by an editor of mine at the BBC and her predecessor. They'd stayed in touch over email for months, happily nattering away, and then they had this idea of a drink for everyone. Great. Only, the editor forwarded around that last email, the one with the invitation, and did not realise their entire conversation was included beneath it. This time I just scrolled to the bottom to see how long this strangely protracted email went on for, but I couldn't miss that the very last page had both of them bitching about specific people in the BBC.

Want a quick way to make sure you never do that? Before you forward an email, select just a little a bit of it. Then when you hit Forward and a new message window opens, the only text in there will be exactly what you highlighted.

As for sending it to the wrong people, there's not a giant amount you can do about that. And having just mocked folk for doing this wrong, I'll admit to you that I blew it once: I sent an email to someone who was the topic of the conversation. It wasn't pretty. I wasn't clever.

So since then, I do look very carefully at the To: but really, until you make the mistake, you can't force yourself into the habit very well.

You can and most of the time you should hide who you're sending something to when it is a lot of people and when they don't know each other. If you're in a small group, everyone knows each other's address and that's fine. If you're emailing that million people, it's not.

I have a pretty extensive list of the personal and business email addresses of entertainment journalists in the UK because one particular public relations firm always sends emails to everyone on its list and doesn't hide them. Giving everyone these addresses is an embarrassing leak of personal information but also, on some email systems, it is a roaring annoyance because you have to scroll through all those names to get to the message itself.

If you must email a million people, don't put their names or addresses in the To: field. Don't put them in CC: either. Put them in BCC:. If you do that, everybody gets the message and nobody gets anyone else's address nor even knows who or how many others are getting it.

You look too young to know what these initials stand for. It's a lovely thing, though: it's another example of how technology terms stay in the language after the technology has gone. Just as we still speak of taping a TV show when you haven't got a VHS tape machine, so CC and BCC hark back to the days of typewriters. You could buy A4 paper then that came with a front, white page as normal but one or two or more pieces of what was called carbon paper behind it. Anything you wrote or typed on the front sheet left marks that showed up on the carbons. So you'd write a letter, send someone the white page, keep the carbons. Or you'd write it once and send those carbon copies around to several people.

So CC is carbon copy. The CC in BCC is too. But the B is Blind. BCC is Blind Carbon Copy: send a message round to everyone you like but without them knowing they aren't the only one.

There can be only one

All writing is personal and connects only the writer with the one person in the audience. If you're one of a team of ten writers doing a TV series that gets five million viewers, it's still you on your own and that one viewer on his or her own. You speak to someone directly, that's how your writing has its punch and the fact that it's delivered en masse doesn't change that.

This is again where it's really handy that you're a writer because you can connect to people through your emails. So many people write so many emails that are at best a chore to read that one from a real writer sings.

I'm praising you but you get this right because, unlike most emailers, you think about your audience. You're emailing because you want or need something from them, but you appreciate that they're busy people being flooded with this stuff so you are quick and you are precise and you are clear.

But you can be quicker and more precise and you can be clearer. Start by making sure you ask for whatever you need right up front. This is one thing you probably don't do now because it seems obvious that you should say hello and remind the person who you are before you ask them for anything.

You do that. I know you do. If you emailed me tomorrow, I would bet money that you'd start by saying hello and that you read this book. You'd probably – hopefully anyway – say something nice about it.

And then you'd get to the point. You'd ask me what To Do app I really recommend, or you'd ask if you could get a discount to a talk of mine, or you'd tell me you'd found a chasm of a mistake in chapter 3.

Do all of that, be as friendly and polite a writer as you are, but do it in reverse order.

Say this:

> Hello William,
>
> If you weren't sponsored by OmniFocus, what To Do app would you really recommend?
>
> I liked the cover photography on your book, by the way. Much better than the words.
>
> Al Phabet

There's no real difference: you've asked for what you've wanted and you've very nicely flattered me or at least you started to.

But two things. First, I can see what you want right away, I don't have to think about it, I don't have to decode it – you've had emails where you wonder what in the world they were on about – and because it's a clear and obvious and quick task, the smart money says I'll reply immediately with the answer that I'm not sponsored by OmniFocus and that the Omni Group has never heard of me. So if you're on a Mac and iOS, my recommendation really is OmniFocus all the way.

The second thing, though, is more subtle. If someone emails me and starts off saying how great I am and wasn't it crazy, that time we spent together in prison, I'm reading through it faster and faster thinking yes, yes, what do they want? I don't mean to be so rude but there's just something about starting with the bonding flattery that makes me think something pretty bad is coming. Or at least something big.

But if you ask what you want up front and then say all that about Tequila parties and stealing a taxi together, you're doing the same job of flattering me, the same job of making sure I remember who you are, the same job of being friendly, but I believe you. I even enjoy it.

It's actually very hard to ask for what you want at the very start of an email: not because of politeness but because of the technical writing challenge. You can't begin an email with a 200-word paragraph and expect it to be read through to the brilliant punchline in the second paragraph, you've got to get in there with a really clear and quick point. You need to do it politely, you need to convey that you're being reasonable and courteous and that the reason you're asking right away is that you know they're busy. You're doing it because you know they're as busy as you are. You're conveying that you are equals and that this is just a quick something you need. And you have to do all of that without actually saying a pixel of it.

Surely only a writer can pull that off. I offer that it's a challenge even for us, but that example above does it all for me and it's so short that you read it without a tenth of the trouble I had writing it. The reader mustn't ever see the effort writing has taken but that effort is worth it: all the work you put into writing a casual, short opening paragraph on an email also focuses you on what you want.

This sounds all callous and calculating but, again, you're a writer. You know what gigantic differences you make with small choices, with small changes to the sequence of a sentence. All the skill and talent you have with prose, poetry, scripts, everything you write, use it on your emails to get what you need.

It doesn't mean it'll work. Not every time. You'll improve your chances tremendously but there will always be the person you email who just never replies or never does anything. You can't fix their problems for them, but there is one little extra thing you can do that might help you and them out. Make your emails complete.

This is really where writers shine. Be concise, be polite, be all that about asking up front, but also do it in such a way that if someone new were to read this one email from you, they'd understand what you meant and what you want and who you are. Even if you've emailed asking them five times before – frankly, I'd have given up by then but you know what you're doing, you know what this person is like so it's your call – make this one email complete. Equally, if you're doing this as the twentieth message in a long, happy, cheery email conversation, write each message so that it stands entirely alone.

Like one episode in a series on TV or a set of books: you have to convey certain basic information each time and do it so that the person you're emailing doesn't see that you're repeating yourself.

Because.

Let's say a script editor hears from his or her producer that there is a new show being made and at that exact moment, you happen to email in asking about new work. Script editors may be the busiest people in drama, though this is a hot-fought title, but there you are, right in front of them. With one click, they forward the email. Done.

Similarly, you want something they can't do – but the second you ask it, they know just who can help you. With one click, they forward your email. Done.

People do this and you want them to do it, but if they have to prefix your email with a 500-word note of their own explaining who you are, they'll leave it to later. And leave it. And leave it. Whereas, if they read the email and can just immediately, instantly forward it to the right person, it's done. They have a To Do list too and they don't even have to add you to it, they've just done it.

So they win because it's quick and like the rest of us they enjoy getting stuff done, especially when it helps you and it maybe helps that producer. You win because they passed it on, you win because they like you for making it so easy, and then you win because they passed it to the right person. And yes, that person wins because they've been forwarded an email from someone who can clearly write.

My mind is always on the end user of an email I send: usually it's the named recipient but when it isn't, I want the person who does read it last to be able to reach me first. So while I'm not generally a fan of email signatures, I have a few TextExpander snippets so that when I'm emailing a magazine, say, I can tap two keys and have my name followed by something like a link to my journalism. If I'm pitching to a book publisher, two keys and my name is followed by a link to my personal website about my books.

I'll take that moment to decide which signature I want to send you, if any of them. What I've been taking an awful lot longer to do is decide about attachments.

No attachments, not really

An easy one first. Don't ever email anyone a book or a script or an article as a Word attachment. Never send them a .mov video of your short film or favourite cat. Not unless they have explicitly asked you. Not ever.

People don't tend to realise that these things take a lot of space. You've had the thing where you tried sending thirty photographs of your family party to your great aunt and your email software said nope, not doing that, not a chance, far too big.

But what you tend to do then is just work around it by sending one or two shots at a time. Fine, it works, but at the other end, these attachments are piling up.

And most people you email are going to be in companies. Many or most companies have a very tight limit on the space in email inboxes. They have to have: they might employ thousands of people and the space they all use has to be paid for on that company's servers. Many, many times I have returned from a holiday to somewhere like the BBC and found that my mailbox is full. Worse, because it's so full, it's been switched off and I have to get IT to reinstate it. Worse plus, because it was full and suspended, the documents I was relying on getting emailed to me over my break have not got through.

Worse plus still, this has all happened because a PR firm has sent me a multi-megabyte attachment for something that has nothing to do with me. They've sent everyone they can find the most gorgeous PDF and embedded videos about a football team, for instance. I wouldn't know one end of a football from the other and you are now reading the only paragraph I have ever written that had the word in it.

So no big attachments. Attachments can deeply annoy people because they can be extremely inconvenient.

Plus, many firms have email systems that simply block messages with attachments. Write the greatest novel in history, but send it as an attachment and that publisher may never even know you exist.

Except.

I'm really, easily clear on not sending videos and novels and scripts. I'm less clear on something short like a CV. I tend to write emails such that you don't need to read a CV but you can if you want to know a little more about me. There's now a Wikipedia page about me because I write *Doctor Who* dramas and that's proven rather handy because I'm chuffed about it but also because I can point people at it with a link.

At this moment, I tend to be okay with sending a really short, small PDF CV as an attachment. If it's anything big, I find a way to ask first. I have written emails asking if I may send a large file but also included a link to where they can download it immediately if they want. They almost never do and they shouldn't.

Don't click on a download link in an email unless you were expecting it or you know the sender and you know that they sent this, that it isn't spam. It may say it's my great novel but is really a spam link out to some untoward website. I think you're able to cope with seeing untoward websites and just closing them with a shudder, but clicking the link sends a message. Literally. Spammers send out billions of emails and a lot of the address simply don't exist or have changed. Clicking the link or telling Outlook yes, load the missing images, sends a message back to the spammer saying this is a real email account.

Don't even click that link if it gives you an actual, real, website URL. If it says http://www.williamgallagher.com then that looks like it's my personal website but it needn't be. You can write any text you like and make it a clickable link to any site you like, so spammers will routinely show you a real address but have it link to their Swiss bank account or something. So if in doubt – and you should always be in doubt of this kind of thing these days – right click on the link and copy it. Paste it somewhere safe like in Evernote or in the main text of a new blank email. What you paste will be the real link, the real place that this thing is trying to get you to go. On some systems, like Macs or iPhones, you can hover your mouse over the link or hold your finger down on it and you'll get a pop up menu or message telling you where that link is really going.

If that seems like a lot of trouble, it isn't really in practice because you get so quick at doing it. Yet it's trouble enough that many people take the easier approach and simply never click on a link.

So for us, that means links are useless – or at least they are if you think they're just for sending people documents. Even knowing that people won't click on the link, I will still include one for my lovely Wikipedia entry because I don't actually care whether anyone goes to it. The link works but its job is to tell this producer or publisher that I have material and that some fine people have written me a Wikipedia entry.

Consequently, I've really just used those links as an advert and I will get an email back from the producer asking me to send a script as an attachment. Everybody wins.

And you thought there was nothing to emails

Thank goodness for phone calls, right? Well...

The thing with emails is that you could spend a year crafting one before you send it. I suppose you could plot and rehearse and practice every phone call you're ever going to make, but odds to onions something will happen in that call that you weren't ready for.

And then of course there's what you do when someone phones you. You know those people you have to deal with? The people who always want something and they might just pay you occasionally?

Phone calls and emails can be equally bad for how people leave you hanging. When can you chase someone? How can you chase someone?

There is actually one more email technique that will help you with this but it's mini version of something you can do on phone calls and in voicemails. So let's cover all this by picking up that phone and having a natter about *The Curse of Other People.*

Section 5

The curse of other people

Writing is supposed to be a solitary life but it feels less and less like that. It's always been the case that it tends to be other people who pay us money but now we're having to meet more, hustle more and arrange more.

That's just to get the work done. Then when we're doing the writing, we have people waiting, we typically have people like sources or researchers whom we're waiting for. And when we're done with the typing, we're expected to start with the yapping and be our own PR engines getting the word out to people who may be a bit sick of writers forever knocking at their door.

Other people are fun. Drama writing, especially, is collaborative. But not everyone is as productive or reliable as you. If only there were some way that you could tell everyone what a tremendous, transformative bargain this book is.

This section is about handling meetings, pitches, phone calls, social media and a touch more about emails – it's about handling other people.

Chapter 11

People

You're working blind when you are submitting and rejecting material to new people but at some point, you're not. You're working with them. Once you've got a face or even just a voice to a name, things change and you can size them up.

You don't have to: there are plenty of people I've worked with for years that I've never tried to define in my head. But there are others where I've noticed certain things work with them and where certain things really don't.

Everyone's different but everyone is working in similar pressured situations so having an idea how they tend to function means knowing how to best help them. From business lunches to full-on meetings, there are also ways that you can get on with the work better.

Sizing people up

This is the shortest thing I'll tell you. Perhaps because I'm rubbish at it, perhaps because I feel that everyone I ever work with will now be asking me what I think of them, how I think I've sized them up. Let me try to dodge that bullet right now: I don't psychoanalyse you and if you've psychoanalysed me, I'd rather you didn't say. Unless you think I'm going to be a danger to the public, then do what you have to do.

All I mean by sizing people up is looking for how they like to work. I'm sizing up their work: is that better? Safer?

I had lunch the other day with an editor who is great in the moment, clearly enjoys people, likes juggling ideas and the creativity of bouncing something up into the air in a group. I suppose if I worked on his staff, I'd be able to get all this from the meetings they have but as a freelancer, I've learnt that lunch is the way to go. It's hard to get a lunch, hard for both of us to fit the other in amongst everything else and sometimes I feel like I should only do it when I have some particular great idea. Equally, though, coming in pre-loaded with ideas turns a friendly lunch into solely a pitch meeting: no matter that we'll end up nattering about all sorts, the intention would've been to pitch so it's a pitch meeting.

Consequently, even though it makes me a little itchy, I'll sometimes contort my schedule to fit in around getting a lunch with him despite having zero ideas. Because I'll enjoy it – that is hugely important, let's never forget that – but also because in the talking something new will likely come up. And if it doesn't, I feel each lunch comes with a day or two afterwards in which I can phone or email him with an idea.

Then I suppose I get more or less the opposite with a script editor I've worked with for some years and have yet to meet at all. Can't tell you how much I enjoy that work, but I've never had lunch with him and the best I can tell is that emailing him ideas is the thing to do. When we're working on the same project, I find it so intense that I don't have the room in my head for any ideas for the next thing at all, but he is extremely prompt at returning emails and calls. When we're done, my head fills up with the new ideas but I can't reach him anywhere near as easily because he's already working with someone else that intently. So I've tended to email him ever shorter ideas and known that it may take months for me to hear back.

In between these two fellas, there's another one. There's one editor I know who tends not to reply to emails very much but so far has almost always said yes to an idea when I've phoned her. So I phone her.

Actually, I've not met her either. I'm starting to take this personally. So let's talk about when you do meet, when you maybe meet a lot of people.

Meeting one person

Stop being a writer for one minute. Be a journalist instead. So rather than being focused on your own work and anxious about how to pitch it to someone, instead think about them. There is never a reason now to walk into a meeting cold: you can so easily find out a lot about the person beforehand, so do.

You don't need to be creepy about it. But if I'm pitching a musical to someone who has only ever worked on westerns, it would help to know. I'm not going to move my musical from Paris to Texas but I am going to wonder about whether and why they're interested. If I read all this on their regular IMDb entry, I'd look for any hints of news stories that they were looking to move into other genres. Ultimately, I'd just ask them right there in the meeting.

But it's a journalism truism that, ideally, you never ask a question you don't already know the answer to. I think that as truisms go, this one is rubbish: you're interviewing someone to find out about them, not to have them answer certain questions in certain ways. (I did once do a long series of interviews with very, very, very similar companies and where I used to plan out my questions, by the end I was also planning out their answers because there was no possibility that they would tell me anything the rest hadn't.The job became less finding out about them and more finding new ways to make the same material interesting, or at least different to last month.)

However, if you write dialogue then you already know that asking questions does more than ask the question: it tells you a lot about both the asker and the person they're asking. Depending on the context, "Where have you been?" is probably not someone asking for an itinerary, it's more likely to be someone hurt or angry who is really asking "How could you go somewhere or do something and not think of me?"

So in the same way, my asking a producer something like "So you're moving into new genres, right?" does a lot of work all by itself. It tells that producer that I know about them, their past successes, their interests and what they're up to now. It tells them I'm professional: I know my business, I know this business, I am far from being a writer with one script in my back pocket and who is unrealistic about zooming from first draft straight to Hollywood. (The trouble with people who are unrealistic is not that we jaded bastards must destroy their dreams but rather that their scripts tend to be rubbish.)

That one short question of mine also tells this producer that I have something in a new genre. So it's saying we have something to talk about and that can be when we start talking about it.

You can easily overdo this. "So you're having to move into new genres since your last three westerns stunk, are you?" wouldn't have quite the same feel.

I'm not so deep into this research that I've ever bothered paying for an IMDb Pro account but we all create such a wide digital footprint – how's that for a term? – that it takes seconds to learn something about us. In seconds we know whether someone is on Twitter, Facebook, we can see their track record of work, we can probably get a CV from their own or some company website, it's a fair bet we can get a photo.

Then not to sound like Eddie Shoestring or Jim Rockford here, you can learn a lot without the internet. This will sound daft and I'm embarrassed even typing it, but when I sign in at a reception, I take a second to read who else has signed in that morning. I do it because of *Between the Lines*, a 1990s BBC drama created by JC Wilsher, produced by Tony Garnett. There's one scene where police officer DS Tony Clark (Neil Pearson) is doing exactly that, he's signing in and he sees that someone he's due to meet with has signed in four hours before. So when he goes into that meeting and she claims she's just got there a few moments before, we're dramatically ready for Tony to be ambushed.

I've just looked it up and it's twenty years since that episode aired. It's called *Some Must Watch...* and is by Rob Heyland, aired 2 November 1993, and I have remembered it every single time I've signed in anywhere. In those twenty years, doing this has helped me exactly once. But, oh, it felt good that day.

Less dramatically, but also many years ago now, someone once kept me waiting for a meeting so I read the magazines in their reception. Of course the magazines were about their industry and it wasn't a surprise that their company was mentioned in the issues left out on the table, but it was in reading those that I learnt about a new project they were doing. So I was able to ask about it as we walked into the meeting room and it turned out to be her project. It turned out to be something she utterly loved doing and was delighted to be able to tell me all about it.

There are few things as fun and exciting as people who are enthused about what they're doing. You could argue that I'm being manipulative looking for these areas to ask them about – because it is true that enthused people tend to at least be more open to being enthused about your ideas – but then you could also argue that I'm losing precious minutes of my meeting to an idea of theirs that I'll never have anything to do with.

When I'm meeting with one person, nuts to productivity and schedules and a stopwatch on the meeting. I'm obviously hoping to get some work from you or to pitch some idea at you, and I have to be aware that you have a schedule but you are my schedule. So long as I'm not outstaying my welcome, so long as I'm not being rude about taking up your time, I'm good. This meeting is the most important part of my day – even if I have four meetings, each of them is the most important – and I enjoy them.

Whereas meetings with lots of people, those aren't so great. Not always.

Meeting with lots of people

I have had a pitch meeting that grew. My agent and I were due to meet with one person and when we got there, he'd brought in someone else. And then during the meeting, a third person arrived. Soon afterwards, the three of them decided they wanted a fourth and a fifth person there, so they got them.

That was great. That was people liking me and an idea of mine so much that they were mentally racing ahead to what they'd do next and who'd be needed for it. So in that case, I was ecstatic that the meeting got bigger. It clearly meant the meeting was going great.

As it happens, yes, I think it was. But the project died within days. So great meetings don't necessarily mean anything at all. But they mean more than bad meetings do.

Usually the only time I tend to get into large meetings is when I've already got the gig and it's a production meeting of some description. But when you're working in a company, you get staff meetings, board meetings, you get meetings about meetings. Depending on the size of the company, you can often get meetings where the real purpose of the whole thing is just for someone to be able to say that you'd had the meeting.

So here's the thing. If any meeting, of any size, is specifically to do with you and your ideas or is a forum where you can pitch yourself and your ideas, treat it as if you're meeting with just one person. Focus like mad, prepare the bejaysus out of your material and don't go in there cold: know something about everyone you can. Just get their job titles straight in your head because it'll help you remember who said what.

For any meeting that isn't about you and your ideas or is just something you have to do as part of the company you work for, the very best thing is to get out of the meeting entirely. You'll rarely manage that, but each time you do, it's worth it. Because there is just no doubt that your time is better spent on your work than in a meeting listening to people not make decisions.

If you're running the meeting, it's easy to fix this: just make decisions. You know how efficient people circulate an agenda beforehand? Nuts to that. Circulate what it's really about instead. So not:

> "Item 1. State of play with new vending machine"

But instead:

> "Bert and Sally to report on vending machine repair"
> "Group to decide on Mars bars versus Twinkies"

Be specific about your meeting and you'll get specific results including the most usefully specific result of them all, which is that the meetings will be faster.

You can only dream about that for meetings being run by other people. But you can do certain things to make them more productive for you and for them.

If you're charged with reporting on something you're doing, take five minutes beforehand to look at your To Do list. Everything you've ticked off is what you can say you've done, everything you haven't is what's left. And the next action is the point you're at right now. Since you write your To Do lists as if someone else were going to do the task, there's no thinking required: you don't have to translate your list of calls into something meaningful, you can just say it. I'd summarise rather than detail, but in this case you can go as deep or as long as you like: you've got all the information you need.

When you do have to report on something, the odds are that you're going to be told something to do next. Take notes. Always take notes: the very dullest, most stupid, most pointless meeting goes faster when you're scribbling down all this rubbish. And the very best, most useful, most significant meetings go better because you're capturing everything you'll need to do.

But do this when you're scribbling. In your notes, there will be points you've got to do, actual tasks. In amongst all the writing about everything and everyone else, there will be tasks that you personally will have to do as a result of the meeting. Mark them in some quick, easy way. I tend to just do this:

--Phone Sally re price of paper stock

Two dashes at the start. Takes a pixel of a second to do. But then immediately after the meeting – immediately, I'm not kidding – I'll go over those notes and pull out everything that begins with two dashes. Those go on my To Do list. If I'm doing the minutes for the meeting, I'll do the same for everyone else. So I'll do the minutes the way that everyone does the minutes but when I email them around, I'll also have a list of each person's tasks after it. I have no idea if it helps them, but it helps me.

As ever, software helps everything. Meetings are delicate things but if you can record them, if you are allowed to, then do. Absolutely the greatest boon to meetings has been the kind of application that records audio while you make notes – and links the two together. I've been using one called SoundNote on my iPad for years and I stick with it because of this linking. It means that when I look at my notes, I can tap a finger on any sentence, any word, any part of the notes and the audio will leap straight to that moment.

So I can see the tasks I've marked out with my two dashes and, if I need to, I can listen to that point in the meeting.

It's fantastic when you can do it, it's no use at all if you're not allowed to record audio.

But I do still make written notes in SoundNote or, more recently, in Evernote. Evernote will record audio too but it doesn't do the linking business so I tend to use it only when I'm not allowed to tape a meeting. I prefer Evernote to SoundNote in part because whatever I write on my iPad in that meeting will already be on my Mac in my office before I've left the room. And it'll be on my iPhone. And if I'm having a chat with someone in their office after that meeting, my note can be on their PC if I want.

Software and services are a whole other subject in productivity, and this would be why they get a whole other section, but just for an example, here's the one other thing I do after meetings. It will sound crazy, or at least absurdly convoluted. But I've started telling you now, so.

I'll copy all the text in SoundNote or Evernote, paste it into a temporary note and delete everything that doesn't begin with two dashes. I end up with a list of tasks. I copy all of that and paste it into an iOS app called Drafts and then I tap a button to send it all to OmniFocus.

Next time I open my To Do app OmniFocus, there are all the meeting tasks in my inbox. If I have five, if I have twenty, they're all in there in one go.

It takes pretty much infinitely less time to say this to you than to do it.

Honest.

But back to normalcy. And back to every type of meeting, no matter what and no matter who it was with.

Afterwards

I don't care who is supposed to email around the minutes of the meeting or write any follow up of any kind. You're going to do it. If this is a big group company meeting and there is someone officially doing meetings, be careful. If it's anyone else's meeting but yours, be careful. But it's easy to be careful, you just do this:

> If it's your meeting or you're doing the minutes, email everyone

> If it's not your meeting, only email whoever's it is

But you're going to email. Asked or not. Because it's that important. It's always that important but important isn't strong enough a word when this is a pitch meeting and you've just agreed to do something or they've just agreed to look at another idea.

With an ordinary meeting, just do that thing I said above about pulling out your tasks and, if you've got to do the minutes, pulling out everyone else's too. Do it immediately, if you can. Do it very bright and early the next morning at the latest. I do think that you're building a (correct) reputation for getting stuff sorted out if you respond quickly and efficiently with all this stuff but that's not why you do it. You do it because if it takes you an hour to write up a meeting right after it's happened, it's going to take you two hours to do it when you've waited a week.

Doing the minutes right afterwards is an exercise in writing quickly: you hardly have to check your notes, you rarely have to play back that audio if you've got it, because the whole thing is in your head. Or at least it all pops back into your head as you read your notes. In a week's time, you won't remember so instantly and it will take time thinking, listening, or even asking people. So the most efficient thing you can do for yourself is do those minutes immediately and it turns out that is the most efficient thing you can do for everyone else to.

Everybody wins, and it costs us nothing.

It's similar for pitch meetings. But here you're doing it for you. If you've had the very best meeting in the world and you bounce out of that room excited that you've been commissioned for a searing warts-and-all dramatic exposé of the entire fishfinger industry, take one minute to write an email. The script can wait for one minute. Because it's shockingly common to find that your commissioning producer also bounced out of that room, was also excited, but believes you're off writing a slapstick farce about cod.

You and your producer are not going to have a great morning if you email and discover that's the misunderstanding. But you aren't half going to have a worse time when you've written 120 pages of script and your producer has lined up funding from every comedy channel in Europe.

On balance, pitch meetings tend to work out for me: by the time we've got to a meeting, I've demonstrated whatever they like and they're actively looking for something. But it's common to find that we end up with something other than I went in for. It can often also happen that we don't get something, that we don't get anything. Instead, I get encouraged to submit something else.

That's good enough for me.

It's good enough for the obvious reason that the door is still open, that they're keeping that door ajar for me, but also because it means the next step is up to me. Yet again, this means there will be a next step because I will take it. You can't make an editor or a producer take the next step that could lead to your working for them, but you can make yourself do it. And very easily.

If coming up with a new idea is easy, anyway. I haven't entirely got that one licked yet.

Meetings during the work

Again, I only tend to get meetings at the start and end of a project unless it's something where I'm working on staff or in someone else's office. And I like that because meetings take time away from the keyboard.

But they do have the advantage that they keep everyone informed. Even if you've sorted out that whole farcical cod misunderstanding at the beginning, it's good to keep checking. It's not going to be that your producer has again misunderstood and is off looking for investment from the Fish Authority. But that producer is as human as you are and after a few weeks of you being quiet because you're writing, they are going to wonder. They must. They can't help it. And worrying is bad because without new material to work on, without new information, our worrying tends to get into a cycle. It becomes the grain of sand that we worry on up into a very polished pearl.

So find an excuse to email or to phone them about a fifth or a quarter of the way through to your deadline. Finding that excuse makes you work, makes you think about what you could possibly ask and that can make you get that much deeper into the writing. It also makes you work in general: you can't dig deep into a feature or a script or a novel if you haven't even started it yet. All of which would be a good enough reason to contact them: it focuses you so it helps you. But it also relaxes them.

And you're working with them partly because they're paying you but mostly because they get stuff made. They know what they're doing – or I've been extraordinarily lucky so far – and so they are useful.

An aside. I have once had a director who didn't know what he was doing. I swear to you that his primary dramatic need was to get the show over early so that he could catch his bus home. There are few people I don't like, there are even fewer who make me angry. But he was one and I am forever grateful because while it means I am unavoidably cautious with each new director, everybody since has been fantastic. And I've appreciated that, I've appreciated them that much more for having seen it done badly.

It's not like there's a tradition in writing to blame your director or moan about your producer, but we've all heard bitching and we've probably all done it. I did know someone who was ecstatic at having got a particular scene past her producer and even as she said it to me, I felt this was probably not the way that drama ought to work. And then I saw her scene in the final show and it was not worth the effort. I'm not knocking her work, I'm not criticising the show, I'm saying that it was the most trivial of scenes in the middle of her story and it was done with the most perfunctory direction because that's all it needed. Anything more would've been startling overkill. But she'd fought over it where I wouldn't have even noticed the opportunity for a fight.

We writers in our silos can think we're on our own because we are. But, most especially in drama, we are working with other people and we do better because of it.

Not to turn this into a diary but to try giving you some balance against that scene-fighting situation, one of the very greatest writing experiences of my career and my life involved no writing at all. Or rather, I'd done the writing and then there I was at the Birmingham Rep watching my actors and my director working on the piece. Drama is collaboration and as intensely, deeply enjoyable as writing alone can be, getting a story on its feet with a cast and director is fantastic.

I'm also going to directly and specifically state here, in case any of them ever read this, that each person I've worked with has been very smart and productive. It is definitely true there with the Rep, it's certainly true with *Doctor Who*. And I love that I get this opportunity to tell you that.

Much as we don't think writers get enough credit, there are plenty of people in drama who get even less and having the chance to mention them is a treat.

But if it's true with them, these people I've most worked with, it is not true with everyone. Now I need you to go all passive-manipulative on everyone you work with.

Train everybody

If you weren't before, you are productive now. And maybe nobody else is. Actually, nobody has to be: certainly, nobody has to be productive just because you or I need them to be.

It's not half a help when they are, though.

When you're doing that meeting email where you state you're going to discuss which confectionary goes in the vending machine, instead of just having a vague agenda item about lunches, you're doing a lot of things. One of them is that you are quietly showing you mean business. You're telling people what you need from them, what they're going to be doing.

But just by doing this, you are also showing that you need them to mean business too. And without ever actually stating so, you're saying that this meeting is going to get something done.

Since you then demonstrate that by having the meeting and having it get something done, everybody believes you that much more next time. Odds to onions, the people in your meeting will eventually start doing exactly the same for their meetings. You'll never get any credit for it, but every meeting will be more productive, every meeting will start to have a point. And that invariably helps you at the very least because they're faster and you can get back to your writing sooner.

Similarly, your email a fifth of the way through the project won't just relax your producer or editor or colleague, it will show them that you are doing the work and they will do the same. If you want it and encourage them to, they'll start keeping you informed with everything too. You might prefer to be locked away writing and keeping the business out of your head, but I believe that communication helps everyone. I do talk a lot, though. so it might just be me

I do also do this very bad thing I mentioned before of replying immediately to emails, if I possibly can. It's partly me, partly this business of dealing with things as they come in – doing it, filing it or deleting it immediately – but I have inadvertently taught people to expect instantaneous replies from me. I like them. It's fun talking. But it kills your writing.

So I've been switching off email, I've been only allowing myself to even read new emails at the top of the hour. And slowly this has changed how people email me. I don't get so many occasions where they've emailed me because that's faster than looking something up for themselves.

I miss it a bit, actually. But my productivity has shot up and most things I write are published so I feel like its worthwhile productivity. It's not just word count for word count's sake.

What I won't waver on is replying at some point and hopefully very soon. Definitely, definitely, unquestionably, if I've promised to email you back by a certain time, you will get that email and it will be on time, it will have whatever I've promised to do.

I don't really see why it shouldn't. I do say no now to a lot of things that I know I can't do or that I can't get done in time. Actually, a quick aside:

> Say no if you have to. But it's better to say, truthfully, that you can't now. If they still need it next Tuesday, then you can take it on.

No matter how polite you are, no is not a word that people like to hear. But even though this next-Tuesday reply is saying no, it's actually telling them a great deal: you're busy, yes, but also that they and what they want done are important to you. They're important enough that you're telling them your situation straight. You're not fobbing them off, you are instead revealing your slate to them and myriad implications start with how you trust them, how you rate them as being as professional as you are – thereby saying you're professional – and that when you do work for them, you will do it seriously. You won't say yes unless you can do it and you won't take on other work if it conflicts with your commitment to them.

So maybe that helps. But also, if I've promised you then I know what I've promised, it's not like there's a problem working out what I've got to do. Writing is hard but knowing what to write, when you've already said what you're going to do, that bit is easy.

You can't make the hard stuff go any better or faster, but you can bat the easy stuff back so I do. What I can't do is look at a deadline and somehow calculate how long something will take me and therefore work backwards to the day, the hour, the minute I should start writing. Instead, I tend to start as early as I can so that I have as much time as I can and so I have the time to see how it's all going. If something goes very badly wrong and takes a lot of effort or time at the start, it's hard to tell someone there's a problem. But if something goes mildly wrong and takes even a little effort, it's geometrically harder to tell them that it's going to be late because you didn't start it until yesterday.

With writing comes deadlines. They just don't have to always be real ones. If you're given a deadline, you're given a deadline. If you're not, offer one. Whether they say yes or just something like "ah, there's no deadline, just do it when you can", use that deadline you just offered. Stick to it.

Always and again, when you deliver on time you look great and it may even be the single best reason why I keep getting hired. I can't speak to whether my work is any good or not, but it is there on time and as silly as that sounds, it is immensely important.

Nonetheless, if you haven't already guessed this, every deadline is a lie.

I know this, I've lied.

A lot.

About three weeks into my first job as a magazine features editor, I learnt to lie and I have not stopped since. Sorry to say this to you as you're a writer, and really sorry to say it because I am too, but writers are unreliable. As an editor, you have an actual, real, solid, immovable date when the project must go live or must go to press, and you give your writer that deadline only if you are the incarnation of insanity. Instead, you give them some other deadline, as far ahead of that real one as you can. Without exception, something will happen, something will need to be discussed with the piece. With some exceptions, this is the horrible moment when you discover that cod farce debacle and have to get another piece written at the speed of light in order to make the real deadline.

So all editors lie to their writers. But if you, as a writer, take away from this that deadlines are lies and that you can stretch them, please picture me slapping my forehead. The point of knowing this truth is not that you can use it to get yourself some extra time, it's so that you understand the pressure that person is under when they set you the deadline.

And knowing that, you know how delivering on time is a balm. Do what you say, when you say you'll do it, and you'll get to do more.

Easy to say

You do have to work at working and there are writers who simply don't like seeing their art or craft as a work skill. Or as a a marketable skill. I won't ever criticise that, all writing is personal and all writers are different, but the odds are you're better than that because you're reading this. I don't think you'd have got very far into this book if you weren't looking for ways to get more writing done and get more time to write.

I like all this stuff because some of it stretches me as a writer – crafting those pitch emails is one thing that has taught me to be clear and concise, at least when I want to be – but mostly it's just such an awful lot easier than writing.

It's ridiculous, really, how simple and small steps now can have big impacts later. But the unpalatable fact is that so many of us writers are so unreliable yet also so precious about our writing that someone who does the work, has the ideas, and understands their business is a boon.

It is a business. Even if you write, say, literary novels and you take, say, ten years to do one, then at the point you're finished and are trying to get it out to people, it becomes a business. You've been away off outside the harsh world while you've been writing but now you have to pay attention to the demands and the rhythms of the novel publishing industry.

Which may mean compromise but it always means two specific things. First, your industry is in trouble. It always is. They always are. Second, there are patterns and schedules in your industry. There are times when it's great to pitch, times when it isn't.

Those dates will change, but not very much. So you have as much notice as you want of when they are and when you need to be ready. Whenever you learn of a date like a commissioning round, just write it down.

Write it down in what is called a tickler file. I swear I'm telling you about these because I like saying the name: tickler file. This used to be done in one of those concertina-like folders that went in filing cabinets and stretched out to have sections for different things. The most common things were months: you'd have one concertina file with sections for January, February and the rest.

I came along a little late to use these as the norm but if I were ever to use an actual tickler file, what I'd do is pop a note in whenever I came across a date or whenever I worked out. BBC Radio 4 has a certain date by which producers must pitch their ideas, for instance. So I asked producers and I worked backwards from there to the time of year when they start finishing the last set of programmes and are looking for ideas for their next round. That's the date I would put in my tickler file.

As it is, I don't have one. I've had exactly one concertina file in my office, ever, and it was more an antique curiosity. As you may well has expected or presumed or assumed, I do have ticklers and I do have them all in software.

I do everything in software. Join me. Join me.

Chapter 12

Own your calls and emails

Some people find it hard to make phone calls, myself included. But every writer finds it hard to handle the fact that people just don't call you back. You have to return their calls and emails, you have to be responsive, yet they don't.

And if you'd just admit it to yourself, you know you wouldn't either. There are reasons why people don't respond and most of them are completely reasonable. But they're so reasonable that they're predictable and that means you can deal with them.

If you or I phone an editor, we know that we will probably get their voicemail and we know to leave a polite message saying who we are, what we want, and including our phone number. Even though we know for certain that editor will never call us back, still we politely leave that same message each time and then we go into a waiting pattern.

Depending on your nerve, your age or your blood pressure, sooner or later you give in and call them again. You feel terrible. You feel like a failure and you do it even though you still know you won't get them and they won't reply.

Change your training. Change the rules. Just a little bit.

Do everything exactly the same but in between leaving the message and hanging up, say exactly this:

> "But it is me wanting to bend your ear, so I'll just try you again later in the week."

You've done the polite thing and all you've done now is add a personal note that's cheery, friendly, acknowledges that they're busy and also lets them off calling you back. This may seem a bit counter-intuitive since you want them to call you back, but since they weren't going to, you've lost nothing. And you've gained that you're not another thing on their To Do list, you're not another demanding writer. Funny thing: you are. You're completely upfront that you want something and that you're going to call back until you get it. But doing it this way, you sound reasonable.

You sound professional.

This is another time where I feel I sound all cold and calculating but the thing with being professional and being nice is not only that it tends to work for you, but it's professional and it's nice. Frankly, it's also easier.

That ear-bending sentence did two more jobs. The big one is that it falls to you now to make the next call and this is exactly what you want. But the smaller thing is that it doesn't tie you down. I hesitated over saying "I'll try you again tomorrow" because I've done that, I've said it, and it works. But I keep saying editors and the like are busy people: aren't you too? You don't want to be so busy tomorrow that you physically can't call them and so look bad for not picking up the phone as you promised. By just saying "later in the week", you've got room yet you still own the conversation.

This is the thing. Own the call, own the email. Make it so that the next move is yours because you can control that, you will make the next move.

Similar with emails

It is the same with emails. I find it harder to slip that idea in, that I'll email again, though. So unless it feels natural, I leave it out and act as if I'm assuming they will reply. But once I've sent it, I add a task to my To Do list to chase it in a week, a month or whatever feels right.

Only, I don't write "Chase so-and-so", I write "Find a peg to use chasing so-and-so".

Peg is a journalism term. It's a thing that you hang a news story on, as you hang a coat on a door. Probably the most common peg in the world is an anniversary but a peg can be any excuse you like that means there is some reason to do the story now. I will work like mad to find a peg. Sometimes I'll even find the peg for chasing someone before I've emailed them the first time. If I've got a play coming up, for instance, I'll know I can use that and I might hold off mentioning it. So in a week or a month, I email them again and just say that I wanted to tell them that I've got this thing on at this theatre.

Usually when I do that, I don't even mention the thing I'm chasing. You don't have to so unless it feels natural or unless your peg has something to do with it, don't bother. You can mention it next time. And there will be a next time.

And a next. Eventually they either commission you or you get a rejection. I did once make a final, I'll-give-up-now call to a magazine asking about an idea I'd pitched months before. Not only did they tell me I got the commission, they told me I already had. And that it was due at the end of the week. If you're thinking I'm twice as efficient as them for how they hadn't bothered to tell me and yet I managed to get the feature in on time, you're wrong. I am more than twice as efficient because I did that, I got it on the deadline and then they had to drop four pages from the issue and bumped me back to the next issue.

I never got another commission from them. At least, not that I know about.

No matter who you are or how often you've been rejected, a rejection comes at you like a slammed door. It feels like the end of the conversation because usually it is exactly that. And while many rejections are really shrugs, some are not and you kinda have to pretend that they all are. If you couldn't give a monkey's about being rejected and you say so convincingly enough, it's not going to help the next time you barrel up pretending to be really keen.

So rejections take a lot of effort either way: getting over the upset if it's big enough or pretending to be upset-but-professional if it's small enough. And while you're doing all that, you're missing the chance to take some control of that rejection. You've owned your calls and emails up to now, you can still do some good with a rejection.

Once you know how to get rejected.

Chapter 13

How to get rejected

This isn't about how to write so badly that you get rejected. It's not possible to write so poorly that absolutely nobody will ever publish you and if that weren't true, we wouldn't keep getting books by [REDACTED AS PER MR ARCHER'S LEGAL SETTLEMENT]. Instead, this is about what to do when you are rejected. It's how to best deal with rejection and it's how – sometimes – you can make it a good thing.

Let's not get daft about it. A slammed door is a slammed door. But just often enough, there is something more and the rejection is the first step rather than the last hope. I've even pitched things knowing that it will be rejected because it was useful for me to do that. Also, I'm an idiot.

We all get patches where it feels like rejections are our sole form of social contact. And there is no writer who hasn't had that slap after slap. You'd think that you would get inured to it and often enough, you do. There's still the one where you really wanted it, where you reached somewhere new and deeper inside yourself to produce some writing that then gets scrunched up by an editor.

Most rejections you get are trivial. Most rejections you get are nothing to do with you. Some of them are entirely your fault. Just as I believe that the best thing a writer can do to learn this craft is to commission other writers, so it's also useful to reject some. It's easier to say this than to get you into a position where you're commissioning and rejecting writers but I have done it, let me show you what happens.

I was features editor on a computer magazine, years ago, back when there were computer magazines. Can't remember how long I was there but it was a while and I used to get quite a lot of unsolicited submissions. Writers I'd never heard of sending me articles in the hope that I'd – well, actually, it's always in the hope that I will hire them rather than use that particular article, but it's what you do, it's how you pitch to a mag. Or it was with us.

Two hundred people sent me articles cold. I'm guessing now, I can't remember but it was around the two hundred mark.

I'll tell you now, I needed writers. I really needed writers. Every month I'd end up learning the most complex and frankly ditchwater-dull topic because I couldn't get anyone else to write something useful about it. And I had the budget to hire people. I did hire people. There was a pot of regulars, there were writers I sought out, and then there were the new ones like these.

I can see it in your face that you're expecting some bad news here so, yes. Of the two hundred people, I commissioned one. Not one hundred, one. Just a single writer out of all of that. He was a nice guy, the article he did was fine. He didn't get a second commission but mostly because he was writing in a really, really specific area and I just never came back to that topic while I was features editor.

While I would rather have commissioned many more, I think the really significant figure is actually seven. That's how many of the two hundred manuscripts that I even read.

Before you go off me forever, I swear to you that not only do I expect I'd do the same again today, I guarantee that you would have done it too. And you would still do it.

Follow. Some of the manuscripts were handwritten. This was for a computer magazine so you really needed to have a computer and if you did, you didn't handwrite copy. You never handwrite material that you're sending anyone anyway. Personally, I can't compose with a pen and I can't read what I scribble anyway so I'm biased, but I don't matter: it is a universal rule that you type.

So all the handwritten ones were gone instantly. They're harder to read, there's no time to retype it for you, and you can tell me you're a writer with lots of experience but if you're not typing, you ain't. Can't afford to risk a big feature on a writer who's never been commissioned for anything at all before. So why read it when you know instantaneously that you will never hire that writer?

Another surprising number included a letter saying that the writer has studied my computer magazine and written this fashion piece especially. Gone.

They always say they studied the magazine. But at the time we ran features that were at least 5,000 words long so if you send me an allegedly fully-finished article that was really half a page of handwriting with spelling mistakes, gone. Without being read.

So many of them, 193 of them, gone before I even read a page. So many reasons but always the same result. You could want me to be fairer, you could want me to read everything, but this is not a competition. It's not a game. It's a job. My role was to get those features into the magazine. No gaps. No blank pages.

And the thing to remember is that this is not about you, it is not about writers at all. Magazines, theatre, books, film, radio, TV, they are all about the audience. Writing is for the audience.

So as writers we do need our talent and we do need our art. We need something to say or there's just no point, but you're not writing to have written, you're writing to be read. You're writing for the audience.

And when we take rejections personally, we are forgetting that our producers and publishers are working for the audience too. You get a shorter chain of people with novels than you do in radio or TV but it's still a chain where all of us are working together to make something for an audience at the end.

You and the producer and the director versus the audience. I'm telling you to remember that but plenty of producers and directors don't. They think it's about them and you won't change their mind. You can't control the editor who believes their project is a world class drama production when you know it's going to end up cancelled on the BBC iPlayer. You can't help but be frustrated by publishers who think that because they don't happen to like this piece, they will never like anything you write. And, more, that this means you are a bad writer. Not a different one.

I did once get the same script rejected twice on the same day. One was from a producer who hated it and slammed the door saying I just couldn't write. The other was Verity Lambert. If you don't know her and you search Google, it's going to tell you first that she was the original producer of *Doctor Who*. But she was so much more. She was a hero of mine for Euston Films and plays like Jack Rosenthal's *The Knowledge*. She's the one who refused to make Lynda La Plante's *Widows* unless the scripts were changed so that the widows got away with their crime. I got to meet her a couple of times quite soon before she died in 2007 and it was a thrill.

She read a piece of mine and she rejected it. But she advised me on what to fix and she listed for me the many things she had liked. The Other Producer hadn't given me any advice but she had given me a list of the many things she disliked so much.

It was the same list.

I'm telling you now, I laughed. And I got really cocky. VERITY LAMBERT. I was damn right to be as pleased as I was.

But I was damn wrong to ignore the Other Producer.

As her rejection was pretty strong and as I knew Verity was this television drama legend, I ignored the Other Producer and I think now that I effectively slammed the door in my own face.

Not sure I'd have liked writing for the Other Producer. But I'd rather have that be my choice later than a door-slam decision now.

What I should've done is what I've done every time since and what I'm going to tell you now. Here's the summary: you can't control other people being wrong but you can control you.

Take control

Understand this first: you will never change a no into a yes. What you might be able to do is change a goodbye forever into a well, keep in touch, okay? And that can be enough.

George Clooney had a nice line about how he was okay about failing in auditions:

> Actors tend to get in their own way, a lot. A lot of times you will do things that will screw up your audition process. I was very bad at auditioning, and I always went in to it saying "God I hope I don't

screw this up." But at the same time, the directors are saying, "God, I hope this person is the savior." You have to remember is that the worst thing that could happen is you don't get the job you don't already have.

If you get rejected by someone, you may be wasting your time trying to keep a line open and working to turn that around. If you don't try, you are definitely wasting your time.

Here's a right stinker of a rejection. It's hopefully far worse than you will ever see in reality but when you first read them, all rejections sound like this:

> Dear Writer,
>
> The standard of scripts was so high except in your case. Yours stank. I mean, for God's sake, an antelope? As the hero figure in a soap opera?
>
> Maybe in Hollyoaks. Or Days of Our Lives.
>
> But here in the real world, take your script and shove it. I know you're disappointed but get used to it. You shouldn't be a writer, you aren't a writer, you're never going to be a writer.
>
> At least, not of the calibre our audience demands for Total Wipe-out: The Movie
>
> Tom E. Producer III

Be careful. Walk around the block and read it again. Even today I got a rejection I thought was nicely worded but final yet as I went to hit Reply, I only then spotted a last line that was offering me something else. And last week I came within a pixel of turning down a job I wanted because I misread the date and thought it was when I was committed to something else. You can call me stupid and I will not disagree, but don't you be as stupid as I am.

Nonetheless, you have to reply to rejections and this is how you would do it for that antelope example:

> Tom,
>
> Thanks very much for letting me know so promptly. You're right of course that I'm disappointed because it is a tremendous project you've got there.
>
> But what you said about the problems of making an antelope be the hero is really smart: I hadn't seen that and I'm going to have to think about it.
>
> Good luck with the show: it's going to be great and I am so looking forward to seeing it. And hopefully we'll get to work together some time: perhaps if I have material I think might be right for you, I can send it over.
>
> Cheers,
> Al Phabet

I think it reads a bit crawling. Tone is very hard. But this is someone busy who thinks they've dispensed wisdom at you and thinks they deserve to be thanked. And it's someone you might want to work with later. Plus, you can put too much effort into these things. There's a line somewhere between being a pro and being unproductive.

So what exactly does this response do?

"Tom". Why not? Usually they call you by your first name, do the same. They can't fire you. They've already fired you.

"Thanks very much for letting me know so promptly". It says thanks and it gives a reason; otherwise no matter how you're slicing this, you're actually saying thanks for rejecting me and that's going too far. Promptly is a good one because it implies efficiency on their part, implies that you notice this and so implies that you are the same. Frankly, unless it took them a year to get back to me, I'm going to say this.

"You're right of course that I'm disappointed because it is a tremendous project you've got there". If you'd got the gig, you'd have said it was a tremendous project. So say it here and you're really saying that you aren't folding your arms and sulking. That works if you're pitching to join something existing, a running show, or something. If it's an original that you've sent in and they've sent back, you say something similar but about them and their production firm.

"But what you say..." Find one thing, one nugget that you can talk about. Don't say they're right, do say they're smart. You're saying that they know their job, you're not saying you'll change anything. "I'm going to have to think about it." You've given me useful points.

"Good luck with the show". Funny one this: you're being nice but in an odd way, you're also keeping yourself at the same level. You're a pro, this is a show and you just don't happen to be working on it. You're working on other ones. We're all professionals here.

"Perhaps if I have material I think might be right..." The most important line in the whole email. Notice that you don't ask permission to send. You don't expect a reply to your reply. You don't want a reply to your reply. You've just arranged not only that you will send more material, but that you can.

Don't send for ages, though. Don't send anything remotely the same as the last material. And do think twice about sending anything: I'd have to really want to work with this guy before I contacted him again.

But I have made it possible. I always do. It is always automatic. It is the point of replying so professionally.

But

I really don't have figures for how often this works or what proportion of rejections I have turned around into eventual commissions. But I do have the statistics on the number of times I've succeeded when I didn't reply to a rejection like this.

Yep. It's that number we all owe ancient Indian mathematicians for: zero.

I said that I've sometimes pitched knowing that I would get rejected. It's pretty rare, but there are times when it's a good idea.

First, I've applied for jobs like editor or features editor of magazines even though I actually wanted to stay as a freelance writer. But the application gets me through the door and in front of all but one of the people I need to impress to get any work. That one remaining person is whichever applicant gets hired. They are the most important and you don't even know their name, but you know for certain when they're going to start. Give it a couple of weeks for the interview process, then a month while they serve their notice at their last place, then ring up and ask for the new editor.

Either they want to bring in new blood to show that they're taking charge or they're so flustered at the million things you have to do as editor that they'll listen to their publisher when they're told you were really good at the interview.

It doesn't always work.

Twice now I've got the job.

The second sort of time that I will pitch to fail is when I really don't know and simply cannot find out enough about a person or a firm to know what opportunities there are. In that case, I'll give it my best shot and wait for the rejection. Then I'll do the kind of reply I just said, wait a few months, and then send in something else that is now that much more finely targeted at them.

It's a long game, clearly, and it only works if you keep doing it and constantly have work out there or are constantly at some stage in the cycle.

But that's the job. And it's also the big advantage: if someone rejects me today, there is work out there with someone else that I can elect to focus on until I stop wanting to bite my keyboard about this one.

Don't ask for feedback

I do sound as if it doesn't matter what the rejection is, I definitely sound as if I barely pay them any notice. What I don't do is get too upset about them. Sometimes, yes. If it really mattered.

But what I also most certainly do not ever do is ask for feedback. If you and I were working together and you hated my writing, of course I'd listen to you. I work with a script editor who phoned me up once to laugh at how bad a scene of mine was – and I laughed with him because he was right and because I knew we'd fix it together.

It's only when I get a rejection email or letter, that's when I don't ask and don't consider asking. Because at the very best, it's a waste of time. And at the worst, it's damaging.

You may have been rejected because your work isn't good enough but if that's true, nobody's ever going to give you a point-by-point analysis. There are so many more reasons to be rejected that statistically it's not all that likely to be your work per se. And if the studio just got another script they fancied more, if they've just gone bust and can't afford to film the project at all, they're not going to tell you anything.

You're probably not even being told about the rejection by the person who rejected you. Odds on, the email is written by an intern whose job today is to email the 70 writers the producers rejected last week.

They won't know the reasons and if it is the producer or publisher rejecting you, they most often won't say the reason. If you catch someone in the right mood, they might feel pressed into saying some nonsense like "the lead character's motivation wasn't clear toward the end". They feel they've said something useful and you've now gone off to rewrite the ending and it's entirely likely that they didn't even read that far.

Save yourself the trouble and also think of that producer, think of that intern: be the one writer who's nice about all this. Steven Moffat had a particularly good line in *Press Gang*: "It's nice to be smart but it's smart to be nice".

It's also just easier. See a rejection as personal and you get tied up in knots; ask them for feedback and you get tied up with the reputation of being a whiner – without getting any advice that was of any use to you. Either way, you get tied up and the whole point of this book is to show you how to be more productive.

So be more productive by being nice about the things you can't control and putting your effort and your time into the things you can.

Section 6

Time off is vital

Apparently.

Section 7

Make your computer work harder

At a stretch, you could do at least something of a To Do list in your head. You definitely only need pen and paper. And apparently there have been calendars and something called appointment diaries for quite some time now. The Romans spelt it fIlofaX.

So if I told you that I had spent – no, I can't do it. Can't. I just started to add up the cost of my computers, my phone, my iPad and as I was going pale I realised I was only adding up the cost of the current stuff. I've been through a lot. I've paid my dues. And subscriptions. And contracts. And loansharks.

Even if I can't face totting it up, we can very easily agree that it is a lot of money and that compared to the cost of a Biro and a sheet of A4 paper, it is ludicrous.

But trust me, it is vital.

Look at it this way. I drink a lot of tea, I mean a huge amount of tea. I am a tea jenny. I don't think you're shocked that I'm part man/part caffeine, but with great tea consumption comes great responsibility. Real men can handle their tea without spilling but I need a little help sometimes. That's especially true when I'm overloaded with caffeine and for those days, I get help from my fantastic cup holder.

It cost me £7,000.

It is a £7,000 cup holder.

You read that right. And people say I spend a lot on Macs.

But it's truly worth it. It can handle tea, it can readily take a flask. If tea is no longer enough then it will equally well hold a can of Pepsi Max or it can even – without any adjustments or adaptors – let me pop a takeaway coffee in there too.

Oh, and it comes with a car.

Also, I have this gorgeous bed that is especially gorgeous at 04:59 in the mornings but admittedly did cost me about the same as a house. Pretty much exactly the same as a house. You'll never guess why.

My point is that going out to buy a lot of hardware to run your To Do list would put a bullet in your finances and actually I think you'd be lost in what to use next. Yet if you already have a computer – and you're a writer, the odds are a bit high that you do – then you already have a calendar and you may already have a To Do application.

This section is going to fill you in on what you might already have and what you can get for free, cheap or bleedin' expensive. Just as I say you shouldn't try to do all of this productivity stuff in one go, you definitely shouldn't try to get and use all of this stuff. I haven't.

There are PC things in here I'd never heard of before writing this book and there are some software applications that I know people rave about and that therefore you might love so obviously they're included – but I don't happen to like them.

Software is made by people and it tends to be like a living demonstration of the way they think. Yet there is this assumption that we have to learn to use software, that you have to study the manual. I am fine with it when you do, I am more than fine with putting in effort when it benefits me, but somehow there is this unspoken, unthought assumption that therefore the software is always right and we must learn how to use it, we must adapt to it.

There was a version of Microsoft Word once that had no visible way of opening a document or creating one: if you foolishly decided you wanted to do such a strange thing, you had to learn a new way and find a new place to do that. I remember wondering when I'd be forced to upgrade to that version and then one day, walking in to a big BBC Worldwide office, I heard this ordinarily calm fella BELLOWING and I knew. Tell me that software is always right. And while you're at it, tell me how Microsoft spent a fortune on user testing yet didn't find a test user who wanted to open or create a Word document. Where do I apply?

You can see the annoyance in me and if you've never felt it over software, you will. This stuff gets deep into us, most especially writers, because we practically commune with it. I can't write on paper, I can't create on it, I have to knead the keys and do so in a word processor. When it does what you need and does it so well, does it in just the way you know is right, then software is the greatest boon to writing since language. Equally, then, when it's ill thought out or when it simply doesn't suit you, it cuts startlingly deeply.

You'd think someone would mention this to software reviewers. Any reviewers, really. Me, for one: I've been as guilty of this as anybody. Intellectually, I know that the software I use may not be right for you but you've already wondered if OmniFocus pays me. And Angela can't exactly complete all my sentences but she very wearily does when the last word is going to be "Evernote".

So software is important and if the applications you use work the same way you do, fantastic. If not, you will spend your days battling this stuff and wishing you'd bought something else.

That is going to happen to you and I can help a bit, but I can't prevent it. I know I only seriously used two different To Do applications on my iPhone, for instance, but I tried upwards of twenty. Right now I'm trying a couple of different calendars, again on my iPhone, but I suspect neither is going be quite right for me.

And then there's the fact that software dies. It always has – in the 1980s and 1990s I was utterly life-support-level dependent on a pair of applications called Now Up-to-Date and Contact but you can't get them any more and the old versions no longer run on current hardware. But the death and life of software is much more important now because we are all so much more connected: we can and so we do put gigantic amounts of data and information into software products. Think what you'd lose if Facebook collapsed tomorrow.

You're also thinking nah, Facebook's not going anywhere. But have you even heard of CompuServe? In its day, it might as well have been the internet. Today, it might as well be fiction. (It does still exist, but is unrecognisable from its glory days.)

Then Google did some rug-pulling when it closed down a service I was going to recommend to you and that I used at least daily, sometimes closer to hourly. Google Reader was effectively a way of getting websites to send you their latest news articles rather than have you keep schlepping around them all. I used the bejaysus out of that and did so from around 2005 when it came in – pretty much destroying all alternatives because it was better at the job and it was free – until July 1, 2013, when Google switched it off.

There are now new alternatives and I am going to show you those because the benefits of reading the web this way are tremendous for research, for fun, for just not taking so much time finding things.

But I had a lot of websites and news sites listed in my Google Reader account and though I've moved to one of these new alternatives, I had to remember to get my list of sites out of Google Reader before they closed it down. At least they gave us notice, at least they gave us a way to get those lists out in time. Not everywhere does. Actually, Google wasn't really a mensch either: by pulling its RSS service it also, as it turns out, severely, radically, near-completely reduced the usefulness of Google Alerts. The company neglected to mention that quite so early.

So you have to think of the future and how you'll be sure to keep all your information. You have to think of the short-term and how you'll back up everything so a nicked phone, a broken iPad or a lightning-struck computer are only painful insurance jobs, not the end of your work. And you need to get software that is right for you.

Backups are down to you. I used to use what I called a bucket under the stairs: it was an Apple Time Machine that all our computers connected to and backed up hourly. Now I pay an annual subscription and our most important computers are backed up online. There are many options but just promise me you'll look into it. I don't want you being productive and then losing everything you've produced.

So while you put off looking into it – I'm not picking on you, I prevaricated too and I did lose some work – let's look at getting you the right software.

In the next chapter, I'm going to work very quickly through To Do software and calendars. As important as these are, as crucial as they are, they're too personal to dictate choices. However, quite brilliantly, you are almost certain to already have one or both of this type of software. And then I suppose there is an argument that if you've already got a free one, there's no reason to ever buy an alternative but I suppose that argument is bollocks. Nonetheless, the only way to find out if software is right for you is to try it and discover what you like, what you need. So maybe the existing free stuff will be all you need and probably it won't but certainly it'll let you test drive the category.

Next, a slightly longer chapter on word processors and the like. You already have one and I don't see that changing to another will make you more productive. But there are different types and they don't only handle the words: so this chapter is about when it's worth it to you to swap to, say, Scrivener for its ability to handle complex books. Or when the cost of Final Draft will seem cheap for the time it saves you fiddling with screenplay formatting and lets you crack on with characters talking.

Then there are services where you buy some software (or get it for free) but the real value is in what that application brings to you. So for instance there's a free iPhone app called Evernote which, like a thousand others, lets you jot down notes. Fine. But Evernote is more useful because it's also a service: write that note down and it is immediately saved to the Evernote company's servers like an instant backup. Great. But Evernote is screamingly useful because you can have apps for it on your phone, iPad, PC, Mac, pretty much anywhere. Make a note on your phone and when you pick up your iPad, that same note is already there waiting for you. There are many such software/service combos and I'll take you through a couple of the most useful for writers.

Last, a chapter on what I think can only be called utilities. Little tools. Tiny, piddly things that you don't think you need but which you then can't fathom how you did without.

I said this right back in the introduction but I need to underline something. I use a Mac and the greatest, most useful Mac software that genuinely transformed my working life means squat to you if you're on a PC. Equally – I presume – the most useful and life-transforming PC software won't help me. Neither of us is going to change our whole computer just in order to load up a To Do app. So if I promise that I'm not interested in trying to get you to use a Mac just because I happen to use one and I don't have the patience for Windows, will you promise to accept that I can't give you specific advice about PCs?

With only a very few exceptions, everything you'll read in the following chapters will apply to both PC and Mac. I've made sure it does. Equally, iOS and Android, the same. There are no easy equivalents either way, each platform has software the others don't but then they also have much in common.

You may have gathered that there is a lot to say about software. There's a huge amount because it is hugely useful for productivity. Funnily enough, though, I can tell you everything you need to know about hardware in one paragraph:

> If and when you can, buy a computer, a smartphone and a tablet.

Okay, call it two paragraphs:

> I have a Mac, an iPhone and an iPad and as fast as each makes me, as productive as any one of them makes me, it's the combination that kills. I'll tell my iPhone ideas and tasks and thoughts as I drive, knowing they'll all be captured and waiting for me when I'm home. I've sometimes started a blog on my iPhone while waiting for a Chinese takeaway and finished one client's article on my iPad while stepping onto a train to get to a different company. The words are just there. I think I'd left the blog in mid-sentence but just carried on typing the rest when I got back to my office Mac.

One more:

> I had a meeting just last week where I suddenly and unexpectedly needed some facts and figures from notes made at a completely different meeting months ago. I hadn't brought the notes, but because I'd made them in Evernote on my office computer, I sat there in the meeting, opened my iPad and simply read that old document as if I'd been brilliant and brought it with me.

But you see I'm already blurring the line from hardware into software. Let's go deal with software then.

Chapter 14

To Do apps and calendars

If you don't already know, it is somewhat surprising how many To Do apps there are for phones, computers and tablets. If you do know, then what's surprising is how many more of them seem to keep popping up.

It's not quite the same with calendars as they are less of a hot potato industry but still you're going to spend some time looking for the best one for you.

To Do apps (task managers)
I'm not kidding: there are myriad To Do applications for PCs, Macs, phones, tablets, everything and they are all the same but they are all different. One will irritate you and the next will be a Godsend.

But the Godsend ones are truly worth it. I found mine after a lot of searching and it was transformative. You wouldn't be reading this book today if I hadn't bought OmniFocus. Not because I told Siri on my iPhone to add a reminder to "Write a productivity book" but because without that system, I wouldn't have my system. I wouldn't be coping. In the introduction, I mentioned that Angela said I now seemed lighter even though I was working more and in much more complex ways. I put that down to OmniFocus.

Don't take this as an advert for the Omni Group's software. No, I've written them an even more fulsome and equally not-paid-for advert in *Next Crisis*, the section on what to do after you've read this book. Instead, take it as an advert for how important the right To Do app is. Important. Crucial. Transformative.

When something is that important, that crucial, that transformative, it's worth spending time and money finding it. I don't regret the money I've spent on To Do apps over the last – gulp – twenty years. I wouldn't regret spending more, I'd just be surprised if I had to. No, wait, hang on: at the time of writing, the Omni Group is working on a new version of OmniFocus for Mac and it's such a big update that it will be sold as a new application. I'm sure there'll be some discount for existing users but I almost don't care: I'll take the discount if I can get one but I'm buying that new version.

I alpha-tested an early version of it a few months ago so I'm sold on it but actually, I was theirs already. That's how valuable the software has been to me. That's how much I trust it. I trust it so much that I inescapably trust the company. I like them so much, I just bought their OmniOutliner product.

You're going to enthuse about your pick as much as I do about mine. And since I've bent your ear off about mine, I'd enjoy it if you did the same with me. Tell me what you went for and why: I seriously doubt you will ever prise me away from OmniFocus but I'd have a very good time hearing how you're having a very good time.

And I can help you narrow the choice. Even though the final decision will be hugely personal and may take you a long time to make, there are certain baselines that you'd need a bleedin' good reason to ignore.

Such as what machines a To Do app runs on.

Hardware for your software

I know you love your phone, I love mine, but even though you can get thousands of different To Do apps that only run on our phones, don't. If it solely runs on phones and not, say, on tablets too, ignore it.

Much as I live in my To Do app, if I had to find my phone and launch the app every time I thought of a task, I'd go spare.

Especially, most especially, if I thought of the task while I was at my computer. It's insane to have this machine in front of you and yet have to go off to find my phone.

Ideally, you need a To Do app that runs on your phone, your tablet and your computer – and where each version talks to the other. If you add a task at your desk, you want it on your phone when you're outside.

If you like the look of an app, search its developers' website for details of its sister products. If there's one there for your computer and tablet, great. If it explicitly says you can run them all together, fantastic.

I used to belong to an app called Appigo To Do and I can't remember now if it ran on anything but iPhone when I started using it. I do know that over the years, it has expanded so that there is an iPad version, a Mac one and an online website-based version. That last is particularly good because it means you can run your Appigo To Do list on any computer that has a web browser and an internet connection. There's an Android version at least in the works too.

That's better than OmniFocus which solely runs on Macs, iPhones and iPads. So there's an example for you of when the specifications don't give you the answer: Appigo To Do has better specs, runs in more places and I liked it very much but I eventually moved to OmniFocus because it suited me better.

But I wouldn't have gone if I couldn't sync my To Dos.

Syncing

I add most of my tasks on my phone as I race around. But I actually do more of them, I get more of them done on my Mac in my office. And when I take the time to review everything and see where I've got to with my myriad To Dos, I almost invariably do that on the iPad. All of which works for me, all of which makes sense, but none of it would do either if the three OmniFocus versions didn't talk to each other.

And this is really important: if they didn't talk to each other automatically. I shouldn't have to do something to make them keep up to date because if I have to do it, sooner or later, I won't do it and it just won't get done.

Exodus

I don't think there's anything to beat trying out a To Do app. Look for free trial or Lite versions if you like, but I'd spring 69p for a new To Do app any day.

But along with trying out some or many – you'll never try them all – there comes the fact that you've got to get your To Do tasks out into the next one. That's another case where a specification is important: you want the To Do app you're trying now to be able to export all your data to let the new one pick it up. Ironically, when any app, not just a To Do one, can export like that, I am significantly more likely to stick with it and never export anywhere.

Apps don't like sharing data, or rather manufacturers don't, so you may have to get used to copying out your tasks into the next app by hand. But look for whether the app has OPML export or import, it'll help. Dropbox syncing is another good one.

But you're looking for me to recommend some software aren't you? Okay. I don't think you'll be shocked that OmniFocus is in my list but depending on your needs and your hardware, this is where I say you should look.

All prices are as at the time of checking. Use a service like AppShopper.com to track when prices rise or fall. Note that many prices are in US dollars because that's how they're sold and that's how you'll buy them, wherever you are. Some developers will convert to your currency as soon as they twig where you're from, others won't. Where possible, though, I've given the official UK price as that's where I'm sitting right now.

OmniFocus
Mac: $79.99, iPhone: $19.99, iPad: $39.99
www.omnigroup.com
If you can only buy one, buy the iPad version. It's by far the best. The iPhone one is great for adding stuff as you run around and I used it by itself for a few days before caving in and buying the other two versions. The Mac one is the most powerful but, as of this writing, it's also much harder to use than the rest. OmniFocus for Mac version 1 looks rough too: it's very old-fashioned and tough to figure out. It's really powerful though and I'm glad I learned how to use it.

But OmniFocus 2 for Mac is coming and I've been testing that for months: it's powerful and much more obviously easy to use. Buy OmniFocus 1 for Mac now and you'll get version 2 for free when it's released.

But that's only the case if you buy from developers: even though OmniFocus for Mac is on the Mac App Store, don't buy it there. You get the same price now but better upgrade details direct from the Omni Group website. And if you got to the Omni Group site, you can download a trial version of the Mac one to use for two weeks.

Note that OmniFocus does not run on Windows but, wherever you are, whatever system you're using, you can email tasks directly into it.

This is handy if I'm using someone's PC but then it's also a thing of beauty whatever I'm doing because I get so many emails that have tasks in them. Get the email, forward it on to my To Do list, sold.

Things 2.0
Mac: £34.99, iPad: £13.99, iPhone: £6.99
culturedcode.com/things
I tell you, this one looks very good. I tried it out on my Mac around the same time I was considering moving to OmniFocus. On the Mac it certainly looks a lot better than OmniFocus but, for me, it just didn't have the oomph.

I do like the name Things, though. I'm a sucker for a good title.

Reminders
No link for this one and no price either: if you have an iPhone, iPad or Mac, you've already got this for free. It's basic but it introduced the concept of location reminders and I have no clue how I coped before those.

Outlook
PC: £109.99, Mac: £142.64 approximately
office.microsoft.com
Never used it. I have actually tried, but it just irritated me. But if you like Outlook for its email, you already know that it is an extremely powerful piece of software and it may suit you to have all that power focused on your To Do lists too.

It's not so powerful and not so great that I think even its fans would spend over a hundred pounds buying it just for the tasks. But you can get it in combinations with other Microsoft products such as Office and in fact you may already have a version of Microsoft Office that includes it.

Appigo To Do and To Do Pro
From free
appigo.com
Runs on Macs, iOS, Web, Android. The website has a page explaining the

differences between the two versions and the prices of all its flavours. It boils down to this: you can pay once to get an app that does a lot of things or you can get a subscription that gives you more.

The killer feature for Appigo To Do, though, is its website and not all the versions can use that.

Remember the Milk
rememberthemilk.com
From free to $25/year
It has the best name of them all and it works across iPhone, iPad, Android and Blackberry as well as online on the web.

Very nicely, you can tweet your task to a certain account and it will be automatically added to your list.

Other stories

I don't actually know how many To Do apps there are in the world and I have tried. But I just tried the Mac App Store and it has 75 in there.

You're sick of me saying it's worth the trouble and it's worth money and it's yadda, yadda, yadda. One more time? Yadda, yadda, yadda. But there is also this:

> Using any To Do app is better than not using anything.

And specifically:

> Using any To Do app is better than pen and paper.

Calendars

There's got to be a computer out there somewhere that doesn't have a calendar. And if you can find it, well, leave it alone.

Given that your computer so nearly certainly has a calendar, I think the solely sensible thing to do is to use it. Use the one you've got until it doesn't do something you need.

The kind of thing that they often don't do or which often send people off buying other ones, though, include basic functionality and sheer speed.

Calendar Functions

It's not just whether they do this but how: is it a doddle to see what you've got on your calendar for the whole of next week? Next month? When you add a new entry, how much faffing about do you have to do? At first, nothing's too much trouble because there is only so much you can possibly have to do: time, date, title, location. But after a few months of using it, you'd be glad of something that can understand when you just type "Lunch with Sally at 2pm" and save you some work.

Just as with To Do apps, you need a calendar that you can use anywhere: it needs to run on your computer, your phone, your tablet and for preference on any computer you happen to be passing. If you want it to.

Outlook has an online version that lets you do much of this and it now comes in flavours for Android and iOS if you subscribe to the Office 365 system.

It's not my favourite but a lot of people love it and a lot more have to use it because it's the standard at their company.

Apple's Mail runs on Macs, iPhones and iPads and now comes with an online version that's rather good. At least, the online one is as good as the Mac/iPhone/iPad one but plenty of people find that isn't good enough.

Myself, I keep coming back to it as I try one thing or another and it doesn't quite fit for me.

But you could look at the best-known alternatives for the Mac:

Outlook
PC: £109.99, Mac: £142.64 approximately
office.microsoft.com
Still and always more an email program, Outlook does include To Do task management and a calendar.

BusyCal
Mac: $50
busymac.com
It's like a bionic calendar that lets you quickly add events and also automatically pulls in extras like weather reports. It's really less a calendar and more a nice front face for Mac OS X's own Calendar.

Google Calendar
Free
google.com/calendar
I'm not a fan of Google's applications like Calendar and Docs. It's partly because I just find them distractingly clunky, partly because I'm just sick of Google taking away services that I like. (They only took away Reader from me, but it cut.) But the Calendar is popular and it integrates well with Google Mail.

It's a funny thing but I don't like being locked in to Google's various systems. I find that funny because I'm cheerily locked into Apple's for all sorts of things. But I used to use Gmail for a private archive; I rigged it so that any mail that wasn't sent from me and to that account was instantly deleted. It meant I could just email myself my writing work as I finished each bit and I'd built up quite an archive there. Except, I found out that I was getting Google+ invitations to that address. How? I didn't give it to anyone, I didn't tell anyone I had it, I literally never sent anyone but myself an email from it. But still they came. And people apparently got mighty miffed when I never replied – because my rules automatically deleted the invitations before I saw them.

I'm hoping that one day I made a mistake and logged into Google+ using that archive address and that therefore it's all my fault. If it is, it's still almighty irritating. So much so that I've stopped using that Gmail archive and now instead save everything to Evernote.

And I've not even opened Google Calendar until right now, today, this minute, when I wanted to get you the direct address. It's actually less clunky than I remember Google Docs being. Still a bit.

Chapter 15

Word processors

Once upon a time, every sane person in the world would tell you to buy Microsoft Word and just stomach the price. They weren't wrong. Certainly not about stomaching the price as even when word processors all cost hundreds of pounds, they were worth it.

Today they're cheaper and they're also more plentiful than they have been in decades as the Word grip is being threatened. You no longer have to stomach Word's faults just because its good features are better than any alternative.

I used to get a lot of funny looks when I worked on computer magazines. Once it was because I was in this big, quite macho-serious business meeting and I pointed out that the company's ace new plan to change the production and printing schedule had been done the year before by something like *Woman's Weekly*. I told 'em the story of this thing and how it had failed at great cost for a women's title. I was ignored, the computer mag did the same thing, it failed the same way and it cost the same amount.

If you're thinking that I've remembered this for twenty years and am using this chance to show you that I am petty, yes, you got me. I did also realise then that I was more a magazine man than I was a computer guy, that I was a writer more than I was a computer fan.

The other main time I was looked at this way, though, was when I mentioned that computer mags weren't going to stick around for all that long. This was during their boom time in the 1990s and now I look like a soothsayer for how they all vanished. (Although currently they're all back as app mags or Android and iPad magazines.) But I knew it would happen because all this had happened before and all this would happen again. What I'd found out when I mentioned this to my colleagues was that there used to be a slew of magazines with titles like *What Fridge?*

Fridges went from being these expensive and even exotic commodities to something you just plugged in and forgot. So whatever tremendous buying and using advice *What Fridge?* used to give you, it stopped being needed.

My beat on computer magazines was word processors. That was my specialism. And I so enjoyed it. I'd write hundreds of thousands of words in every new word processor that came along and it was anoraksic heaven.

You never quite lose the beat, either. So – hang on, let me count – today I have written in three things that you could call word processors. Pages, Evernote, iBooks Author. Each time I reached for the nearest or I reached for the one that would do what I wanted at that moment.

In some deep-down geeky way, I love that. Lots of interesting software to play with, lots of opportunity to write. Is it just me or does your keyboard feel different in any given word processor?

Right, okay, it's just me. The part of me that isn't deep down, that would rather get on with the work than geek out, doesn't like this at all. If I weren't on a Mac where Spotlight will find me anything I've written, anywhere I've written it, I'd have to stop to think each time where something was. Where did I leave off writing that note about a property problem? Where did I put my cue sheet for the teleseminar? I'm having a very bad day: where in the world did I put my own chapter on *Bad Days*?

This too will pass. We're in an interesting stage where software is changing such that we have to think less and less about where we put a document, it'll just be there. But we're also at an very interesting time – for us word processor freaks – where Microsoft Word is losing its stranglehold.

WordStar was beaten by WordPerfect was beaten by Microsoft Word. That all happened a long time ago and Microsoft Word has been the one to buy as much because it's the last one standing as it is for being powerful. There is a huge amount to find extraordinarily, profoundly irritating about Word but it also has some welly under the hood and was oftentimes a good choice for a long and complex document.

Those days of automatically turning to it are gone, however. It's a longer story and I will bend your ear at length if you are foolish enough to ever ask me, but Word's losing its market because the market is changing. That's the short answer. It took five years for Word to make an appearance on the iPhone in any Microsoft-backed form. It took three years for it to make it to the iPad and the only reason it was two years quicker is that Apple released the iPad two years after the iPhone.

Those devices shook up a lot of things and suddenly Apple's own word processor, Pages, became a much more attractive option. It was always good, always pretty powerful and getting more so with each release. But now it was on iPad and iPhone and in very, very good versions that were preposterously cheap.

There are many other word processors on these devices but the fact that they weren't Microsoft Word just helped loosen Word's soldering. And that worked back from the phones and tablets to computers. As soon as you couldn't have Word on the machine you were using, you found you didn't have to have it. Once that happened, once the single most compelling reason to buy Word was gone, it was down to what worked the best. And that isn't always Word.

I still deliver copy in Word to most people I work with but I tend to do it by running the text through Word before saving a version. I write it somewhere else, then pop it in to Word for the last bit. Even then, I've learnt to always save the document as the older version of Word, the .doc one because so many places have not yet updated to the later .docx version. Microsoft switched to this XML file format, .docx, in 2007. And still I find I have to use the older one.

That would've been unthinkable once. I bet Microsoft didn't think people would hold off updating this long. But it's as if the fact that you had to make a choice to upgrade everyone to the new version instead of moving a few staff at a time made everyone stop. You could feel a bit sorry for Microsoft: they made us stop and think and then they missed the iOS boat. If we've got to spend more money than we expected and it wasn't on the machines we wanted to buy, is Word the way to go? And for some people, especially some writers with very specific needs, the answer turned out to be an easy no.

Before your alternatives, though: here's that elephant in the room:

Microsoft Word
From £109.99
PC, Mac, Android and iOS (with subscription)
office.microsoft.com

It is still true that every writer can use Word for every thing. It just might take more work than you're willing to put in when there are options.

Now here are your alternative options.

For all writers

If cost is your big factor, if you like the power and are fine with the complexity of Microsoft Word and its Microsoft Office home, try the free alternative LibreOffice. You may have heard of a free one called Open Office and you may yet see that available to download. I'm sure there are technical differences but LibreOffice span off from Open Office when the older one was shuttered or Bentoed a couple of years ago. There is now a new spinoff from Apache that is also called Open Office, chiefly to confuse everyone. There will doubtlessly be deep-down technical changes but for writers, just go for the one that is currently supported and at least a little established. Right now, that means LibreOffice.

LibreOffice
Free
PC, Mac, Linux
libreoffice.org
An Android and iOS version is at least in the works. There's not a lot to say about this, at least not by me, as it's very much like Word and it has its fans. Plus it's free, so it's not like it's hard to try it out for a spin.

Pages
Currently £13.99 for Mac, £6.99 for iOS (universal version for both iPad and iPhone)
apple.com/pages
Tremendously easy to use and powerful word processor. If there's one I use the most, it's Pages. It hasn't been updated on the Mac in a time and it doesn't work on PCs but both of those things may be changing: as of this writing, Apple is beta-testing an online-only version of Pages.

For some years, in some versions, Apple has had its Mail, Calendar and other applications available online through iCloud but it's now adding what it calls its iWork suite: the word processor Pages plus the spreadsheet Numbers and the presentation software Keynote. All three are very strong on Macs and iPhones and the current beta version on the web is rather remarkable. You could forget that you're using a website, even if you're on a PC.

That is in beta and so not officially available or supported yet but it's surely close to release. There is rumour that when it is out, it will be free to iCloud users. If that hasn't happened by the time you read this, assume it isn't going to.

You can and many people have gone mad trying to predict Apple. I've bought Pages, Numbers and Keynote at full price and I'm fine if they suddenly turn free: I've got great use out of my dosh to date.

Google Docs
Free
PC, Mac, iOS, Android
docs.google.com
A particularly powerful word processor. It's also free and while Google switches off services on a whim, the odds have to be against it ever getting rid of this as it's Google's way into big businesses. I'd have said that Google Reader was safe not so long ago, but.

Google Docs is built to be used by multiple people at once. I've used it when collaborating in a group that needed one single, central document for a job and there we'd all just open it when we needed it, close it when we were done. But you can also have everyone working in it at once. So if you're in a writing partnership, this might be good for you. It might also drive you spare. But definitely try it.

As with Google Calendar, I find it a bit clunky. That's hard to explain and it does seem to look better every time I see that price. But when you have options, remember that you're going to be face to nose with your word processor for a horrific number of hours in your life so liking what you see is a good thing.

Evernote
Free for basic use, £35/year premium
evernote.com
See the chapter on *Services* for writers: Evernote is not really a word processor, even though you can write a huge amount in it – and I have used it for prose as well as meeting notes.

Scrivener
Mac: $45, PC: $40
literatureandlatte.com
A longtime favourite of Mac users, this has now come to Windows too. It is a word processor but it's more than that. It's a repository for what writers need and do: you can have research from the web over here, text that you've written over there, and you can slice and dice and Julienne it all any way you fancy. It has an extremely dedicated fan base and it does come from a firm with the great name Literature and Latte.

For scriptwriters

You can write scripts in anything you like but it's a specialist market where the writers need particular formatting and software companies can smell profit. That doesn't mean that their software is in some way wrong or unnecessary, it just means that there is more scriptwriting software out there than there are applications for haiku poetry.

Final Draft
Mac and PC: $249 (approximately £162)
Final Draft Writer
iPad: £34.99
finaldraft.com
There is also a Final Draft Reader for iPad but it is pointless. It's an app that lets you read scripts written in this Final Draft format. Who just reads them? If you have an iPad and need Final Draft, you're better off getting Final Draft Writer which can read and write this stuff.

The firm calls this the industry standard screenwriting application. (It also does stage and radio plays.) And it's fair comment: nothing else has its prevalence in Hollywood and, at least at one point, the BBC had a special version that it was contractually allowed to give to writers on its series.

It's one where there is good and bad about it, though, and sometimes the bad outweighs the good. That business of it being an industry standard is clearly a good thing but the world seems to be going away from such standards and since anything can shove out a PDF copy that looks right for scripts, the requirement for Final Draft is weakening. Plus there are alternatives that will write to this format for less cash.

You can also tell that it has been the industry leader for a long time and that it runs on Windows and Macs alike; it has the look of a lowest-common denominator application that doesn't exploit either computer platform nor rushes to update.

I like Final Draft but it lost a bucket of brownie points with me for Final Draft Reader: after years of everyone waiting for an iPad version of the app, they released that. More, they said it was because this was what we wanted. Sure, if you ask someone whether they'd like to be able to read their Final Draft scripts on their iPad, they're going to say yes. Ask them if they'd prefer to be able to read and write them instead, you get exactly the same answer yet that yes is 100% different. That spin and some bugs in the first release put me off. But I do have it on my iPad and I do use it.

And I do like it on my Mac. I turn to it to write scripts far faster than I ever do Pages or Word because it does make the job easier.

If you don't yet write scripts, you won't yet get why that's even possible. But, for instance, when you're writing a very strong exchange of dialogue between two characters, it is a boon to be able to hit Return after one speech and immediately start the rejoinder and know that Final Draft will pop the right character names in for you.

I first bought a version of Final Draft a good fifteen years ago and I've probably only written twenty scripts in it – my *Doctor Who* work has to be delivered in Word so I tend to write it there or in Pages – but I stick with it because I have it and what I like about it, I like a lot.

If I didn't have it, I'd spend some time with the trial version of Final Draft and also of the next one: Celtx.

Celtx
Free for basic version, $14.99 for Celtx Plus
celtx.com
The end result is a script that looks like it is in the perfect industry format, so this is like Final Draft but with different buttons and a much lower cost.

Others

Markdown
Price from free (depending on application)
Sites include:
daringfireball.net
This is less an application, more a format that very many software programs work with. It's designed for writers who need to produce text that will go on websites: while it stays out of your way to let you write, it is built to produce website-like coding. So behind the scenes, it is adding in codes to say that, for instance, where you've hit return twice there, a website will need the code "<p>".

You might write for a website and never once know a single thing about the formatting in which case you can write in Word or Pages or anything you like. If you do have to know or you do like knowing, then you tend to like Markdown for its control yet how it's simpler than writing the straight HTML code that is the lingua franca of websites.

Fans of Markdown tend to like writing everything in it. So it has its fans and they are passionate but it's probably fair to paint them all with the same brush and say they might, just might, be leaning a pixel toward the geeky side. If that's you, get to the Markdown website above and knock yourself out.

Chapter 16

Utilities

There are software applications and there's apps and then there are utilities. Three different words for the same thing: how can anyone be confused? It's all software but the habit is to use that term to mean the big stuff like your Microsoft Words on your big desktop computer.

It used to be that a utility was a small, did-one-thing piece of software. That's now pretty much what an app is. Apps began being called that on phones and as it's short for application, the term has spread back to everything.

But for us, let's be pure. We're talking small software tools that help writers.

There is a little problem with talking to you about small tools for writers and that would be the sheer volume of them. On the good side, a stunning number are utterly worthless. On the bad side, it's a wee bit tricky to work out which will be worthless to you and the writing that you do. Plus, there are so many that just listing the things would age us both. And there is this business of how you might love and adore a particular writer's utility but it won't work on your type of computer.

So here's the thing. Please look at this chapter as a guide to the kinds of things that are out there. We'll get specific about particularly useful ones but I've picked things that I use but which are available on PCs as well as Macs – or where I've at least found a similar equivalent.

As with all the chapters here on software of any description, you're going to find that some prices are in US dollars. Isn't it a small world now that you can just buy from the States and download straight to your computer?

1Password
Bundles and deals available but single-user prices are:
PC/Windows: $49.99, Mac: $49.99, iPhone/iPad: $17.99;
Android: temporarily free
1password.com
You're a writer on a budget, you juggle a lot of credit cards. This 1Password keeps all my card details securely and when I'm buying another book that I really shouldn't, two taps of the keyboard and it enters my card number and all details for me.

And that's not what it's meant for.

It's meant for logging in to websites. This 1Password keeps all your usernames too, all your passwords and if you're still using the same one for everything, you'll stop because it also makes creating safer, different passwords supremely easy.

Angela showed me this first on her iPhone and I wondered why anyone would ever want such a thing. Within the day, I'd bought it and moved it to the front screen of my own phone. It's been there ever since and I use it so much that I bought the Mac version and showed Angela. You can't believe how handy it is to tap two keys and have all your username and passwords for a site popped into the right places. Then 1Password even presses the login button for you.

I did find that upgrading to the latest version of 1Password was teeth-pulling-murder on iPhone, it felt more like alchemy than an installation. But when you add it new or just when you have got through doing the upgrading, it's superb.

As of this writing, the Android version is free. It's been free for quite some time but seemingly only while it's in beta testing. So at some point it's going to cost on there too. Have a look at the website for the pricing, though: there are a lot of deals where you get, say, the Mac and the Windows versions together for a good price.

If you use both types of computer, it's obviously handy to do that but the two versions play nice too: you have the same data on both. Add a website when you're on the Mac, add a credit card when you're on your PC and each computer gets what you've done on the other.

TextExpander
Mac: £24.49, iPhone/iPad: £2.99
smilesoftware.com
I actually like typing. But TextExpander helps me type the stuff I want to type by saving me the repetitive stuff. If I've got to tell someone my home postal address, for instance, I now just have to type ";home" – without the quotes but with that semi-colon – and that's all replaced immediately by the full thing. I chose what I wanted to type to have that happen and I keep choosing: my TextExpander collection grows and grows.

Since I started writing *Doctor Who* radio drama, for instance, there's been this Wikipedia page made about me and if I wanted to chuff at you, I now just have to type ";wiki" and you've got the address. Here: http://en.wikipedia.org/wiki/William_Gallagher_(writer). That probably happened too quickly for you to see.

For years people have told me that their Mac feels wrong without TextExpander, that they have to install it whenever they go to a new machine. Now that I use it, I want to tell you that Macs feel wrong without TextExpander, that I wanted to install it at the last magazine I worked on. And I could've done, I had the licence to do it for my own personal use wherever I was, but that magazine company's IT department won't allow any installation of anything. Still, the number of times I would automatically write something beginning with a semi-colon. Thinking about it, there's probably a few stray semi-colons in the magazine now. Cough.

Anyway. What's particularly good about TextExpander is that it works in everything on your Mac. Whether you're writing in Word or Final Draft, even if you're just renaming a file or searching for something in Spotlight, it works. That's why you forget that it's not part of every Mac.

And that's why it's a bit of a jolt when you buy it for iOS: it doesn't work everywhere there. Apps have to specifically allow it to work and while many developers have, Apple has not. So it isn't in Mail, Safari or any of the core apps you get. There is an Apple equivalent called Shortcuts that expands little abbreviations: see Settings/Keyboard. Nobody uses it. Apple barely mentions it and even if you find it, somehow it's a bit of a shrug and for all you intend to use it, you just don't.

Instead, there is a sort-of way to use TextExpander in everything: you go to the TextExpander app, type your little shortcut and then copy out the address or the wikipedia URL, whatever it is, and paste it into whatever else you're using on your iPhone and iPad. It's not great. It's not great at all. But you get used to it.

Whereas TextExpander for Mac is great and you never get used to how handy it is.

There's no TextExpander for PCs but take a look at Breevy over on 16software.com/breevy which is the nearest equivalent I can find. It costs £34.95 for PC.

OmniOutliner
Mac: Standard $39.99, Professional $69.99, iPad: $19.99
omnigroup.com
It's an outliner. You know this stuff, you do outlines. I didn't. Not until I tried this. And, hand on heart, I tried it partly because I like the same company's OmniFocus To Do app so very much. I wasn't disappointed. I was a bit surprised how much I liked it, too. If I look at the outline for this book, I can see that it's very basic and I've hardly used any of the features I've read that OmniOutliner has. So on the one hand, surely I could've done this in Word or even – shudder – on paper. But on the other, I didn't have to learn a whole new application before I could do some useful, productive work.

There's no reason you should know this and there's hopefully no reason you should spot it, but there were some knotty little problems in working out the sequence of this book: I found I'm so naturally drawn to software, for instance, that I would start writing about a particular application in several chapters. Deciding where the best spot for anything was, I got a little lost. It was like I knew I had so much I wanted to tell you, so very much that has helped me in my work from the 5am starts to the TextExpander utility that I had a sea of detail in my head. I got the trial version of OmniOutliner and started bashing in every thought I had. Then I was dragging things around, seeing connections between the thoughts, seeing big gaps where I was clueless about things I knew you'd need to know.

And then as I'd write a section, I'd tick it off in the outline and I'd even change the colour to green. Right now, as it happens, the outline is an ocean of green and it's absurdly satisfying.

Before the two-week trial was up, I bought OmniOutliner for Mac. Actually, I bought OmniOutliner 3 for Mac and there is a version 4 currently in beta testing so then I signed up for that. Just as with OmniFocus for Mac, the currently shipping version – as of this writing – is powerful but looks a bit old and there is a new one coming that is rather nicer. Rather easier to use. Within two weeks of having bought OmniOutliner 3, I was beta testing OmniOutliner 4 and I haven't gone back.

There's no PC version of any of the Omni Group's software. But you can get outlining in Word and a Lifehacker.com poll in 2009 picked Microsoft OneNote (http://office.microsoft.com/en-gb/onenote/) which costs from £109.99 with Microsoft Office. There are also iOS and Android versions that are free. I haven't used it so don't take this as my recommendation for OneNote but do take it as my recommendation for Lifehacker.com: I read that site most days and have done for some years.

Model pictured

Listen, you're getting that I use a lot of utilities but I think you're missing their impact in all this dry stuff about prices and alternative PC versions. So considering that you lost all respect for me right back there when I told you I get up at 5am and keep a Daily Log of what I do, let me pause for a moment and unabashedly reveal how deep is my utility love.

Please just keep in mind that you don't have to do any of this, that in fact it builds to the one thing I said in the introduction that you should ignore me about. Also, normal service will resume in just a moment with the single most useful utility I have ever used.

But.

Deep breath.

Okay, so, I tend to have a lot of nightmares. I'll regularly wake up clutching my chest and sweating. Once I woke myself up from a really bad one, lurched to the loo, went back to bed and fell instantly into a new nightmare that was like The Making Of the previous one.

It's fantastic.

And in the chest-clutching loo-dashing sweat-mopping moments, I will often write down an idea I've got from all this. You're a writer, you know this: everything is material. Only, I cannot handwrite at the best of times so after some years of indecipherable scrawls, I have the solution.

I lurch awake, reach for my iPhone which is acting as my bedside clock (app #1: Awesome Clock). I swipe up the screen to un-dim the screen, then tap LaunchCentre Pro (app #2) and then within that tap a button marked Story Ideas. That launches a little dialogue box wherein I type what I've been dreaming about, then I tap Go and the text I've written is sent to app #3, Drafts. Then Drafts, all by itself, appends tonight's text on to the end of an Evernote (app #4) note where I collect this stuff. Drafts bleeps when it's sent that off to Evernote but usually I don't hear it because I'm already back asleep.

You may well think that this is a bit of utility-overkill and I might agree with you but for the fact that it is a way for me to collect the innards of my fraught head and that has actually led to script ideas. Chiefly thrillers, since you ask, but whatever the genre of nightmare, this cascade of little utilities is foolproof. See for yourself: I saved this one for you. This is what I wrote around 2am one night recently:

> Velcro diving back and changing cabs / this wa NYC – to nor it a piece about a clever guy. Sesilbkikecfokting blossh socks. Hard out oh both and then learn jr tircicajdcuey ybewevedsotibbldubcgojrxto like him http relitinu vyvyririi. Brunch shotgun thin and thr too dyeoyjnydgbkubuktjbour ikeposjinjetevepp I've b

'Course, there was a bit of auto-correction going on there but I think we can both see that there's the germ of an idea in that.

Anyway.

Well.

So back to the useful stuff. I mean it when I say this is the most useful utility I use: it's something that I check on all my devices at least, at the very least, thirty times a day. Remember a moment ago when I recommended Lifehacker.com? Today is the actually first day I've gone to lifehacker.com itself in two years: I only went to check if they'd done anything about outliners for PCs. Usually, I read their site and many, many others through an RSS reader. Get yourself a biscuit and let me tell you about the gorgeousness of RSS readers.

Reeder
Prices vary and many other RSS readers are available
reederapp.com

Reeder is just my favourite way amongst many to read RSS. What you need to know is how fantastic RSS is, most especially for writers and most especially for productive writers.

I'm a news junkie and I particularly love getting different views of the same story. When I was a teenager, I used to read the New York Times every Saturday in Birmingham Central Library because – well, partly because I'm obsessed with NYC – but also because it was dramatically fascinating. If a story about Britain reached the New York Times, you knew it was big. And you could see an entirely alien view of the tale.

I can't remember when I stopped reading it at the library but I read it every day now on my iPhone and I have done so for something like five years. Even before iPhone, I've certainly opened its website as often as I have, say, the Guardian in the UK but the killer for me is this RSS.

The way I work, the things I'm interested in and the way I can use this as a distraction, I could readily go to the New York Times website once, twice, ten times a day. I could go to the BBC News Online site once an hour. Go to Lifehacker. Macworld. Blogs like the one on kenwriting.com once a week for the new entry there. OmniFocus has a blog about updates, I could surely swing by there every few weeks to see if they've got anything new. I read so many news sites, blogs, columns and features that without question I could spend the entire day going from one to the next.

With RSS, they all come to me.

While I'm boiling the kettle, I'll flick through my RSS reader and it will show me that yes, there is a new entry on the OmniFocus blog. I didn't have to go there, I don't ever go there and find that there isn't an entry yet. It comes to me and I can read it right there.

What you get to read, how much or how little of that new article, is up to the news site. Every good news website has what's called an RSS feed that includes at least their headlines. See their headlines, choose whether you want to read on. Some many more include the headline and the standfirst – the bit at the top of a feature that tells you what it's about and tries to entice you to read. Many include the first few paragraphs of the story. Some give you the lot, the entire story

But in every single case you can choose to tap or click on your RSS reader to go through to the site and read it there.

What's actually happening, just so you know, is that each site has its little RSS feed list tucked away somewhere. Each time they publish a new article, they add its headline and link to a wee little file somewhere on their server. When I open my RSS reader, it goes around every site I like looking to see if there's anything new on those wee files and it brings it to me if there is.

I am now vastly more informed and pretty much infinitely more engaged in news than I have ever been. It's a rubbish and miserable time to be engaged in politics, but there you go. At least I am engaged very quickly and if it takes much time away from my writing, it's less because I'm searching my favourite websites for news and more because news of the latest arts cuts have driven me to alcohol.

Reeder is an RSS reader for Mac and iOS. I like it deeply but it is one of many, in fact very many. What it does is search the sites you pick for their RSS feed, brings that to you and when you've read a story, never shows it to you again. Not on your iPhone, your iPad or your Mac: wherever you read it, it gets marked as read and your other devices are told. So I could read RSS on my iPhone in the kitchen, I could have a really good morning-paper kind of time as I lounge about reading on my iPad over breakfast in a coffee shop. And I could take a minute from writing at my Mac to look up the latest headlines. Without my doing much, all the news I want is there. Without my doing anything, the iPad, Mac and iPhone sync so that I never have to slog through a lot of stories I've already read.

Only, there's a problem there. Reeder used to do that syncing of what you've read and what you haven't via a free service called Google Reader. It was free and it worked well and you could read RSS news directly on it but Google Reader was clunky and we all used it under sufferance until Google switched it off and, man, we howled.

Right now, other companies are trying to fill this gap and one called Feedly is doing particularly nicely: it has its own RSS reader that you can run on iOS and on the web, but it also lets other firms sync through it. The developers of each RSS app have to update their software to use Feedly or anything other than the defunct Google Reader and some are taking longer than others. Some are using this as a time to do other whizzy updates. So as of this moment, my favourite Reeder has been updated to use Feedly on iPhone but not on Mac or iPad.

And lest RSS seem a bit obscure to you or website developers, my reading has dropped substantially since this happened. I haven't opened Reeder on my Mac or iPad in months.

But I do still read it twenty or thirty times a day on my iPhone, so.

Reeder and its many equivalents are utilities for Macs and PCs, they're apps for iPhone/iPad and Android. But RSS itself is really a service. The utilities and apps are your choice of tap or faucet where RSS is the water.

The line between software and service is blurring ever more because of phone apps. Good. Services are what your computer was made for. Okay, okay, your computer was made for you to write on. But apart from that.

Chapter 17

Services

This has already happened: the internet is considered a standard for houses just as water, electricity and the telephone are. It's become so integral that we forget and have no reason ever to remember how it's part of everything we do. It's exactly the same for the type of services writers can now get online.

Actually, every single service that is good for writers is good for everybody else but we don't care about them. We care about what helps you write and if there's anything these services have in common, it is the freakily magical way they all let you start a sentence on your computer and finish it on your phone.

If you get confused by anything I tell you here, just wait an hour and it will have changed. We're at a geekily curious time when the whole way we look at how we use computers is changing. Seriously. If you've been using yours for any length of time you're familiar with starting a new Word document, for instance, and then saving it somewhere. You might have worked out a whole system of folders or directories where you bung all your novel chapters in here, your correspondence there, your script ideas somewhere else.

And if you're like me, you hit Save an awful lot. We've learnt to save. I wish I'd learnt to save money as much. But it is a muscle memory now: when I stop to pause for even an instant or for you to get a word in, my fingers have tapped the keys to save the document without my realising. It was ever thus and it will probably ever be thus because it is so ingrained now.

But I'm writing this to you in Pages and it is saving itself for me all the time. I can and I am hitting Save but it doesn't need me. It's saved. Get on with your writing, William. Leave all that saving to me.

Equally, I don't actually know where it's saved. It's somewhere in iCloud. I have not the faintest clue where it is. I just know that the next time I open Pages on my Mac, it'll be there. If I go to my iPhone right now and open Pages, there it is. This document. In fact, hang on –

– hello, I'm writing this on my iPhone in the kitchen. Do you take sugar?

And now I'm back on my office Mac. I brought you a biscuit. I did open and close this chapter on my iPhone but all the way through my kettle journey, it was open here on the Mac. And there it is, half a sentence written downstairs. No saving, no copying, it was just there when I sat back down.

If you're new to computers, you're going to think that this is the way it should work. And you'd be exactly right. But it is so different to the open, save, close, files and folders that have been with us since the 1970s and 1980s that it genuinely does feel like magic.

Soon enough, we'll be used to it and documents will just be there when we need them, wherever we are, and we will just reach for the nearest screen to carry on a thought, whenever we want.

But if that's going to take some of us some considerable mental adjustment, it's taking the same for the entire computer industry. And right now, we ain't there. This Pages stunt – and it does seem like a stunt, doesn't it? – works great over iCloud but I have to remember to open Pages to do it. I can't just open the document, I can't just think I want to add a bit to what I'm telling you about Services, I have to think that and then remember that what I've written so far is in Pages. I have to open the application first, then open the document. And if I should fancy writing on Word in my living room, tough. I can get this document out of Pages and into Word but it takes a shovel. It's nowhere near as magically transparent as it should be.

Also, you've guessed that iCloud and Pages, being an Apple gig, won't work on PCs. So now I have to find the right computer as well as the right application and suddenly all this write wherever you are lark seems a bit bollocks. It's coming, it will be here, we will get used to it and it will be the way that all computers should always have worked, but it isn't today.

But even what we have this very minute is better than we used to have. You can do that Pages stunt and I have sat in someone's office, forced to wait because they're delayed in meetings, and I have opened up this very book to carry on writing. On a PC instead of a Mac. In another city instead of my own. This same type of service is how I'm also able to drag up documents from years ago that I suddenly and unexpectedly need in another town. It's how I can be a bit casual about backups: wherever I write, my writing is immediately also over there on my iPhone. It's in my really nice iPad bag. It's on my Mac at my home office. And my home office backs up online all the time. So while I'm not asking you to nick my MacBook, the truth is that if you did snatch it from me and run away giggling, I wouldn't have lost a syllable of anything I was writing.

Some of that is Apple, some of it is iCloud. But it's also many services done by plenty of other companies that do it for PCs as well as Macs. This is another layer of things to remember: as well as thinking of the type of computer and which application before I can write, I do have to sometimes think about which service is best for whatever I'm doing today. And I use three different services, all of which I'm going to enthuse about to you here.

Take the enthusiasm. Use the services. Forget that it seems a bit rich having to remember three different services in order to be able to write wherever you are without thinking. The first is iCloud and you've seen what that can do. Plus, if you have Macs or iOS, you've already got it. So for the other two, start by doing this:

Get Dropbox

That wasn't as long a list of instructions as you expected, was it? Go to dropbox.com and sign up for the free service.

Dropbox
dropbox.com
Put the iCloud Pages stunt out of your mind for a moment. You use Dropbox exactly the way you have always used folders and files where you choose where to save what and you know where to go get it later. Except that when you have Dropbox anything you save is available to you anywhere. Anywhere in the world. On any device.

Here's what it looks like, what it appears to do. You have a Dropbox folder on your PC or Mac and you keep anything you like in there. Save documents to it, drag photos in, do whatever you would do with any other folder on your computer. There is zero difference between your Dropbox folder and anywhere else on your computer.

Except.

When you go to your laptop, say, there's your exact same Dropbox folder waiting for you. Everything you saved in it on your desktop computer is there. Open a Word document on your laptop, make some changes. Save some music there. And when you go back to your desktop computer, those changes and that music are right there in your Dropbox.

It is the same folder on every machine, everywhere. It looks like you just have this magic folder that is everywhere you go. (Seriously everywhere: you can open that same folder on your phone or on any computer with an internet connection, if you want to. And if you're worrying about the security of having your stuff spread all over the world, trust me. They know what they're doing. It's secure.)

You could leave it at that. You could just know that you will come to forget that you've signed up somewhere, that you're logged in somewhere, you will just come to expect that your work will be wherever you are.

I would rather that you knew what was really happening, how this really works. And what's really happening is that you have some space on Dropbox.com's own servers. When you save something to your Dropbox folder on your desktop computer, the service quietly copies it up to that server. Then when you open your Dropbox folder on your laptop, the service quietly copies down everything new to it.

Even though it does all this without your having to think about it, it's handy to know how it works because the next time you save a video off your camera to your laptop, it is going to take an age to do this quiet copying – because video files are huge – and you'll be wondering why it isn't immediately on your desktop computer. Just walk away and it will happen.

Once you've used it, you'll forget it's there until you hit its limits: you start with a free account that gives you space for a 2Gb folder. (I'd reckon to get three or four hours of video in that space, if that helps.) The next stage is a 100Gb folder but you have to pay for that and it costs about a tenner a month.

Some Mac users do this and put their entire Documents folder in their 100Gb Dropbox. Some PC users put their entire My Documents folder in there. So all of their work is available to them always and everywhere.

And while Dropbox is not a backup service – accidentally delete a file on your desktop and Dropbox will dutifully delete it on your laptop – if someone nicks your laptop seconds after you've finished your fantastic poem, at least the poem won't be lost.

Wherever you go, there your documents are.

Having put iCloud out of your mind, now please put Dropbox out of your mind and do this:

Get Evernote

Evernote
evernote.com
Where Dropbox is for always having your documents with you, Evernote is for making documents. Actually it's for making notes. When the phone rings, for instance, I'll answer it and make a note in Evernote as we talk.

Evernote becomes ubiquitous. Like Dropbox and iCloud, it's another service where whatever you do is always available to you. Those quick phone call notes, they'll be on my Mac where I was when you rang but before I know it and without my actually doing anything, that same note will be on my iPhone before we hang up. It'll be on my iPad if I turn to that during the conversation.

I pile everything in to Evernote. Looking at mine now, I can see a whole notebook devoted to a trip I'm taking to California. All the plane tickets are in there. Hotel reservations. Car details. Itinerary. Stuff I Need to Pack.

By chance there's not a huge amount in my Evernote about this book, I think I just saw this book as my nattering to you. But I recently wrote a 150,000-word book and my Evernote is replete with stuff to do with that project. Many, many phone call notes. Lots of interview transcripts. Some drafts of sections. Collected and collated interviews from old magazines. Scans of articles, PDF copies of scripts.

That's a thought, PDFs. I keep the manuals for my mother's TV set and our washing machine in Evernote: two things I can never fathom without the manual but can never find the manual when I need it. There's a problem with my mom's TV such that it's annoyingly easy to accidentally press the wrong button and switch off her Red Button services – and oddly contorted to figure out the right buttons to undo that. She can't remember the sequence, I can't remember the sequence, so I just bunged the manual into Evernote and get it out the next time this happens. The whole manual is just in there when I need to find something.

(I have scanned a manual before, by the way. But these days it is just so much more easy to type the word 'manual' into Google and add the model name of whatever TV, computer, kettle you've got. I find the manual and download it. I use a Mac utility called Hazel that sees I've downloaded a PDF and automatically pops it into Evernote for me. So it's pretty much zero effort from me, pretty much amazingly useful from Evernote.)

Finding stuff in Evernote is startlingly quick and easy, even when you have a lot in there. Hang on - let me do another quick count. I have about seventy notebooks (just collections of notes on the same or similar topic, like my California one) and it says there's a total of 2,505 notes. Somewhere in there is a Nigella Lawson recipe for ragu and I can find it faster than lightspeed by just typing the word ragu.

The utterly gorgeous or at least nearly utterly gorgeous thing about Evernote is that this ragu recipe is a photograph. I have her book but for speed in the kitchen, I took a snap of that page on my iPhone and saved it directly into Evernote. And Evernote read it. It OCRd the piece – optical character recognition if you care, reading the thing if you don't – and understood that it was a photo of text, so it made a note of the text. That's how I can type ragu and it will find it even in a photograph.

What stops that being completely utterly gorgeous is that you can only use this for finding. I had to ask Evernote support, I was so sure I was wrong here, but no. I can find that ragu recipe in a heartbeat but I can't select all the ingredients text and copy it out to my shopping list. They say it's because their software reads the text word by word and if there's any doubt, it keeps all the possibilities. A word that looks like 'mind' it might actually be 'mine' so they keep both tucked away in case you search for either. If you could copy the text you'd get it but with every one of these possibilities included so it would be near enough gibberish: "I am going out of my mind mine moan Minoan mince".

Fine. Even clever. But it means I have had a great interview for my book scanned in from a magazine and even with it right there on my screen, even with Evernote having found and indexed every word in the scan image, I had to type out the quotes I wanted by hand.

You're not on my side in this, are you? I can hear you saying tough tum tiddly. And I can't disagree. But I do disagree. It was a pain and it took a shine off Evernote for me.

Not enough that I didn't become a premium user, though. For free, you can have an Evernote account – and there are free Evernote apps for Mac, PC, iPhone, iPad, Android, everything – and do what you like with it. Have as many notes and notebooks as you want, knock yourself out. There is a catch and it is a limit but it's a generous one: the limit when you have a free account is that you can't upload a gigantic amount each month. That's all. If you have a lot of PDF manuals you want to keep in Evernote, at most you'd have to wait until next month to add some more.

In practice, I never came near to bursting the limit on my free account. I went Premium because I was using it a lot and think it's a great service, because I wanted certain extras like faster OCR of images that premium users get, and because Angela bought me a year's subscription as a Christmas present. There is still a limit to how much you can upload a month but it's gigantic – and, oddly, now I'm a Premium user with this increased usage limit, somehow I have hit it many times. That's because the more you use it, the more you realise you can use it and the more you come to rely on it. So I pile everything in and when I got the Premium account, I started gathering up all the stuff I used to have lying around like contracts and invoices and bills and meeting notes and chucked them all in.

One month I was uploading so much and I needed to do that rather than wait to the next month to continue, I temporarily bought some extra capacity and carried on.

Evernote is bacon-saving, by the way. When I was in a meeting and suddenly needed notes from a completely different topic, I was Mr Efficient and even Mr Very Clever, because it was there in my Evernote notebook and I found it and pulled it all up as if I'd thought to bring the notes with me on purpose.

There are alternatives to Evernote. Microsoft OneNote is sort of like it. Google would very much like you to use its new Google Keep instead of either. That's the thing they launched the day after announcing they were switching off Google Reader, though, so my ears, for one, went a bit deaf to their extolling how great it would be to keep all your information in their Google Keep service forever.

Basic Evernote is free. Premium costs £4/month or £35/year. Free if you know Angela.

Section 8

Stolen goods

Hopefully you've never heard of this – or if you have, it's less because you're a thief, more because you happen to have done some research into burglary for a book – but there is a thing called a Bump Key. If you're skilled enough, if you insert it just far enough and turn it just so, a bump on the back of the key will open the lock.

I think that's equal parts fascinating and the reason I've put an extra mortice lock on my door. But I can't be entirely against bump keys and grand theft because some of this book is nicked. Most of what you've read is mine or comes from how I've used things and developed them under steam-cooker pressure. Yet there are principles and techniques that I think are key – only a tiny pun intended – and which have helped me so much that I want them to help you too. So here they all are.

David Allen's Getting Things Done book

If there is one thing that made me lighter, in mood and life if not in weight, it was actually a piece of software called OmniFocus. But OmniFocus was designed to work best with Allen's *Getting Things Done* system. So far as I know, there is no connection between him and this software. And I do for certain know that you needn't have heard of this GTD to get a lot out of OF.

But the core ideas that OmniFocus was built to use are just really good. Really clever. Really useful. And they are all from Allen's book. Only, he does have this jargon habit: things you haven't done yet are called 'open loops'; your calendar is the 'hard landscape' of your life. And he wrote the book in 2001: I cannot fathom why he hasn't updated it because things have changed so much that it's like reading a period piece.

This is especially true for writers but for anyone, the world has changed. He writes a lot about dividing tasks so that, for instance, you don't see your work To Do list when you're at home.

He would have you make a separate list of things you can do when you are at your computer. Or how useful it is that you don't see your list of phone calls when you're not at your phone. It's adorable.

But you end up translating the book as you go. Still, have a go or maybe just try out the sample section first from Amazon. I've written a smidgeon more and included a swift Amazon link at theblankscreen.co.uk/gtd

Inbox Zero

This one's been adopted and adapted enough that I'm not confident I've got the original fella but I believe I have: Merlin Mann. He does a podcast called Back to Work which gets raves but I've listened and I think it gets right raves presenting it with him so I've never made it past the kind of zoo format opening. Otherwise, I've watched many a video with him speaking on these topics and he's an entertaining, smart, interesting guy. As I mentioned before, his home online now seems to be the Back to Work podcast that I'm not very keen on. But try it: 5b5.tv/b2w

Mac Power Users podcast

Not a lot of use if you're into Windows but considering that I used to make a gorgeously successful podcast myself, it is weird how rarely I listen to them now. Except this one. I looked up Mac Power Users with David Sparks and Katie Floyd when they were doing a special on something I was interested in. I must've listened to fifty episodes since. It's got so that if I'm thinking about something like outliners and whether they'd be any use to me for a particular job, I'll search macpowerusers.com to see if they've covered it. If they have, there'll be the audio – typically around ninety minutes – and also extensive show notes with lots of links out to the things I'll end up wanting to check out.

Dave Crenshaw

I only know him for the one thing about proving we can't multitask but that was very helpful to me. He has a site at davecrenshaw.com which talks a lot about this and similar ideas.

Section 9

Next crisis

I can't remember what I'd just asked Siri to do but once I was nattering away when my voice must've been really slurring with tiredness. So it ignored my question in favour of saying: "Put down this iPhone right now and take a nap". Wasn't that scary?

It's good advice, though, and you know it is: you just sometimes need telling too. There is always something else to do, there is always another crisis, but there is just one you. The one me currently has a stomach so empty that it's rumbling showtunes. I accept that I need to go eat something. I accept that food is fuel and that sleep is when the office is closed.

Now that I feel so much more in control of everything I'm doing, I'm even starting to suspect that there might be other things in life beside work, food and sleep.

It's just a suspicion, don't hold me to that.

This whole book is about clearing more time for you to sit in front of that blank screen. But time is a tool: when there's a crisis, you know that you could resolve it if you just had the time. Or money. If you could throw money at it, you'd be fine. You can throw time at a problem – if you have that time available.

So as hard as it is to get started on that blank screen and as hard as it is to keep going, it's worth the effort. I said right at the start of this book that nothing in it would improve your writing but I lied to you.

Having more time and having so many of your other concerns and worries dealt with means that your writing will improve. It's you doing the improving, but you have the space and the time you need to do that now.

You know this: the most useful thing you can ever do as a writer is write.

You don't get any work without it. You don't get an audience or a readership. And what's most important, to me at least, is that you don't get better at it. Unless you write.

Now you've got this time, keep it up. Keep doing the productivity lark, keep working away. You're going to go crazy, you're going to walk away from all of this, but you can always come back to it and it will always help you out.

Grief, I sound like the leader of a cult.

Let me race to the opposite type of encouragement then. Let me tell you exactly what to do next.

1. Adopt one productivity technique

You've just done all this reading, you've just bought the whole book, and I'm saying you should ignore every single part of it bar one. It's up to you which one that is, but pick it quickly. Pick the thing that immediately makes you think that yes, I can do that, it will help me.

Pick it and do it. Keep on doing it. At least for a month, try it for one month. Hopefully it will stick and after that time it won't be my idea anymore, it'll be yours. It'll be that ingrained into you. If it fails, try another idea for a month.

And do the same if that works, too. Add these ideas to your working life a bit at a time and they will help.

I've said that I don't use everything in this book. I don't use the Jerry Seinfeld technique, for instance. I'm trying to think whether there's anything else: I'm sure there must be. But it's this business about it being ingrained: I now can't write a bad To Do list, for instance. It might be pie in the sky but you'll know which pie and what sky.

2. Read Getting Things Done

Writers can hold conflicting thoughts in their head so I can say this to you and know you'll understand: I recommend David Allen's book and I don't. See *Stolen Goods* for my reasons.

Still, I enjoyed reading it, I got a lot from it. And it's a book so anyone can get it quite cheaply.

Whereas OmniFocus is comparatively expensive. Nonetheless:

3. Buy OmniFocus

Listen, this is that rare kind of advert: the absolutely totally evangelical enthusing advert that isn't paid for by the company. Or anyone. The one thing that stops me writing you a love letter about OmniFocus is that it only works on Macs and iOS. If it worked for every computer, I'd have gone on about it even more and shown you my OmniFocus friendship ring long before now.

That's despite the fact that even if you have the computer and the phone or iPad to run it, it may yet not be for you. And it's despite the fact that where you can get myriad To Do apps for free, OmniFocus costs.

There are three versions and I bought them all, I use them all, I would buy them all again. I don't want to be too specific because prices vary but, for example, when I bought OmniFocus for iPhone, OmniFocus for iPad and OmniFocus for Mac, the total for the lot was around £80.

If you ask me, it's peanuts. Compared to how much I use them and how much they've helped me.

Advert over. No, wait: the website you require is omnigroup.com. Now, advert over.

4. The cheapest thing you can do

Following the cost of OmniFocus, here's the very cheapest thing I recommend: read this book again. I'd say you'd benefit from re-reading all of Section 1 about the kind of philosophy of all this and then cherry pick your way through the rest whenever it feels handy.

5. Audiobook version

Funny you should ask this right now, but there is a kind of audiobook version of *The Blank Screen*. It's called my coming to your house or us going to an event and in either case, me yapping. I give good yap. And if you want to talk to me at an event or you want to email hello, there's a good chance I can help you out with answers that more specifically fit your writing and your situation.

I do group courses and individual tuition: have a look at TheBlankScreen.co.uk for details of all that.

Section 10

Thanks and other stories

Reading this section is like getting to the high numbers on your TV's EPG: you've exhausted all possible sources of entertainment, diversion or information but you press on because you can see there's more to watch, surely it isn't all rubbish.

It's all rubbish. Except you know that if I didn't include this, someone would object. And not with a tweet – "No copyright page? FAIL" – or a one-star review – "Call himself productive? He can't even produce a disclaimer page" – but more with a lawsuit. "Have you bought a free To Do app on his recommendation and it wasn't your fault? Call 1-800-SUE-HIS-SORRY-ASS. No win, no fee."

So this is the section where I try to cover my back but, seriously, if you're just reading this because it's here, let's just go get a drink and have a chat. (Legal disclaimer: the drink may be virtual and the first round is on you.) The quickest way to cover this is to say you should have a look at my website theblankscreen.co.uk and that'll point you at my email inbox, it'll tell you some more productivity things. Mind you, if those were that great they'd already be in the book.

If you haven't now scarpered off to theblankscreen.co.uk then let me tell you that all of the text in this book was written by me. I also did the design, layout and whathaveyou: what can I say? I'm trying to show you how to be productive.

Also, full disclosure, I only did the design for the Kindle and paperback versions: I started with the Apple iBooks edition because iBooks Author is a very nice application and its sample designs were demonstrably better than mine.

I'm not in any way affiliated, endorsed or even heard of by any of the software companies or other sources mentioned in the book or on the website. It is for want of trying. I've made no attempt to get sponsored or bribed and more than the legal bits, I want you to know this because I'm not kidding about what I recommend. Yet again, if it's a PC thing I'm telling you about then I am just passing on recommendations, I don't know that stuff myself. If it's Mac stuff or it's a service that runs across platforms, I'm recommending it because I've used it and either love it myself or can see and tell you why other people like it more than I do.

All of this software and any hardware or services I mention will almost certainly have trademarks and they are the property of their respective owners like they always were.

I can't take responsibility or liability for anything that happens while you're reading this book or when you're using any of the advice within it. You know that. I've just got to say it.

Whereas what I want to say is: thanks for reading.

And I rush to tell you that while this is written for you, specifically you, there are some fine folk who checked it was good enough for you first. Angela Gallagher, Jason Arnopp, Margaret Foxall, Katharine D'Souza and Steph Vidal-Hall all should've caught that almighty mistake you've spotted in chapter 3. Then Maeve Clarke and Charlie Jordan were invaluably helpful too and all this came out of a chat at *Room 204*, the Writing West Midlands writers' programme that I got on in early 2013. So particular thanks there to Jonathan Davidson, Sara Beadle, Joanne Penn and Sian Buckley plus my fellow writers on the scheme.

ISBN-13 978-0-9926569-1-1

Published simultaneously in the United Kingdom, United States and Canada. September 2013

William Gallagher
Dark Ride, Birmingham, England

6303630R00158

Printed in Great Britain
by Amazon.co.uk, Ltd.,
Marston Gate.